ROBERTSON

Plays by Robertson Davies

Full length:
• *The King Who Could Not Dream,* written 1944, unproduced.
• *King Phoenix,* written 1947, first production 1950. Toronto: New Press (in *Hunting Stuart and Other Plays,* edited by Brian Parker), 1972.
• *Benoni,* written 1945, produced by the Crest Theatre, Toronto, as *A Jig for the Gypsy,* 1954. Toronto: Clarke, Irwin, 1954.
• *Fortune, My Foe,* first production 1948. Toronto: Clarke, Irwin, 1949; Toronto: Simon & Pierre, 1993.
• *At My Heart's Core,* first production for Peterborough's centenary 1950. Toronto: Clarke, Irwin, 1950; Toronto: Simon & Pierre, 1991.
• *Hunting Stuart,* first production at Crest Theatre, 1955. Toronto: New Press, 1972. New edition 1994.
• *General Confession,* unproduced. Toronto: New Press (in *Hunting Stuart*), 1972.
• *Love and Libel,* adaptation of the novel *Leaven of Malice,* Broadway production 1960. *Canadian Drama 7,* no. 2 (1981): 117-190, *Leaven of Malice: A Theatrical Extravaganza.*
• *Question Time,* first produced St. Lawrence Centre, 1975. Toronto: Macmillan, 1975.
• *Pontiac and the Green Man,* for University of Toronto sesquicentennial, 1975.
• *World of Wonders,* adapted for the stage by Elliot Hayes, performed at Stratford, Ontario, 1992.

One act:
• *Hope Deferred,* first produced 1948. Toronto: Clarke, Irwin (in *Eros at Breakfast and Other Plays*), 1949.
• *Overlaid,* first produced by the Ottawa Drama League 1947. Toronto: Samuel French, 1948; Toronto: Simon & Pierre, 1991.
• *Eros at Breakfast,* first production 1948. Toronto: Clarke, Irwin, 1949; Toronto: Simon & Pierre, 1993.
• *The Voice of the People,* first production 1950, directed by Robertson Davies. Toronto: Clarke, Irwin (in *Eros at Breakfast*), 1949; new edition 1994.
• *At the Gates of the Righteous,* first produced 1948. Toronto: Clarke, Irwin (in *Eros at Breakfast*), 1949.

Masques:
• *A Masque of Aesop,* performed at Upper Canada College, 1952. Toronto: Clarke, Irwin, 1952, 1955.
• *A Masque of Mr. Punch,* performed at Upper Canada College, 1963. Toronto: Oxford, 1963.

Television Drama:
• *Brothers in the Black Art,* broadcast by CBC-TV 1974. Vancouver: Alcuin Society, 1981.

ROBERTSON DAVIES

TWO PLAYS

Hunting Stuart

&

The Voice of the People

 Simon & Pierre

General Editor: Marian M. Wilson
Copy Editor: Jean Paton
Printed and Bound in Canada

The publication of this book was made possible by support from several sources. We would like to acknowledge the generous assistance and ongoing support of the **Canada Council**, **The Book Publishing Industry Development Program** of the **Department of Canadian Heritage**, **The Ontario Arts Council**, and **The Ontario Publishing Centre** of the **Ministry of Culture, Tourism and Recreation.**

J. Kirk Howard, President

1 2 3 4 5 • 9 7 8 6 5

Canadian Cataloguing in Publication Data

Davies, Robertson, 1913-
  Hunting Stuart ; &, The voice of the people

Plays.
ISBN 0-88924-259-3

I. Title. II. Title: The voice of the people.

PS8507.A67H85 1994   C812'.54   C94-932729-8
PR9199.3.D38H85 1994

Order from Simon & Pierre Publishing Co. Ltd.

2181 Queen Street East	73 Lime Walk	1823 Maryland Avenue
Suite 301	Headington, Oxford	P.O. Box 1000
Toronto, Canada	England	Niagara Falls, N.Y.
M4E 1E5	OX37AD	14302-1000

Contents

Introduction
by Robertson Davies

As I write this, there is a great deal of indignation in the United Kingdom, and possibly an even greater amount of prurient interest elsewhere in the world, concerning the rowdy behaviour of some members of Britain's royal house. A headline in the London *Times* reads *Can the Royal Family Survive?* and articles and letters everywhere proclaim the opinions of anti-royalists who declare that the money spent on maintaining the Royal Family might better be spent on government committees, pensions for parliamentarians, more trade commissions and goodwill visits by elected persons to countries outside the UK, support for backward countries and all the other things that delight the hearts and raise the spirits of politicians. The substantial amount of money that Britain receives from the Royal Family, from the Crown Estates, is rarely mentioned.

Here in Canada, where we spend no money whatever on the royal family, except when they visit our shores (and the demands of hospitality are, after all, binding) we can be more philosophical about this crisis. But we are a country with a monarchical form of government, the Queen is Queen of Canada, and we may fittingly be interested in what the institution of royalty means in our time, and whether it is worth maintaining.

In a government like ours, the Crown is the abiding and unshakable element in government; politicians may come and go but the Crown remains and certain aspects of our system pertain to it which are not dependent on any political party. In this sense the Crown is the consecrated spirit of Canada. The embodiment of the Crown is the monarch, who has virtually no personal political power, but whose personal influence may be very great, as an adviser to whatever government may be in power. And in addition to this, millions of people have an affectionate regard for the monarch, as somebody above politics who stands for rights and values which the majority of people cherish.

Understandably, when members of the royal family kick up their heels and play the fool (exactly as ordinary people do all the time without exciting any special remark) people who do not separate the constitutional aspect of monarchy, and its mystical significance as an embodiment of cherished rights and beliefs from the fallible human beings who are born into the royal family, or marry into it, think that the monarchal system is tumbling down.

Because I do not think that this is so, and because I think that monarchy has a psychological significance for the countries that maintain it, I
wrote the play *Hunting Stuart* some years ago. It deals with the matters in
terms of comedy, but not mindless comedy – not just for giggles. In it an
ordinary man discovers that he is of royal blood and has a very slight claim
to the throne of Britain. He is what is called a Pretender, in the sense of the
word which means a claimant, one who advances a right to something
which is in the possession of another. When for a time he embodies the
spirit of one of his ancestors, he shows tendencies that shock his wife who
has the not uncommon idea that the monarch is precisely like herself,
though richer. But the pleasure-loving, woman-chasing pseudo-king is
something else; he shows himself truly royal when he cures a suffering
woman by the Royal Touch, which was widely believed in as late as the
reign of Queen Anne (1702-1714) who was the last ruler of Stuart blood.
There is, it appears, something more in kingship than ancestry and privi-
lege; there is a trace of divinity, as well.

Of course the play is a fantasy and a comedy, but I do not think it is
trivial. It was written for the Crest Theatre, in Toronto, where it was produced in 1955, with Donald Davis as Henry Benedict Stuart, and his sister
Barbara as Dr. Maria Clementina Sobieska. They splendidly realized the
saturnine physical distinction of the Stuarts. The play was well received by
its audiences.

Perhaps a brief historical note may be of interest to readers who have forgotten about the Stuarts. They were famous in the history of Scotland from
the twelfth century, and from the fourteenth century were kings of that
country; it was through the marriage of James IV of Scotland with
Margaret, the daughter of Henry VII of England, that the Stuart claim to
the English throne became a reality in 1603, when James VI of Scotland
(son of Mary, Queen of Scots) succeeded Queen Elizabeth I as monarch of
both Scotland and England as King James I. He was not at all a bad king
and we remember him as having inspired the translation of the Bible into
English, which has not since been surpassed for literary worth. But the
Stuarts were an unlucky family, intelligent and refined, great lovers of art
and letters, but absurdly blind to political reality and it was this that
brought James's son Charles I to the headsman's block. After an interval
(1649-1660) during which England and Scotland tasted to the full the
delights of puritan democracy, the monarchy was restored and King
Charles II ruled – and although opinions vary he seems to have ruled pretty
well – until his death in 1685, when he was succeeded by his brother James
II, a disastrous king who had all the pig-headedness of the family with

none of its charm, and who was forced into exile in 1688. After that the Stuarts were wanderers, and pensioners of the French court, though still asserting their right to the throne of Britain. James III, son of James II, is remembered as 'the Old Pretender' (to that throne) and his eldest son Charles Edward Louis Philip Casimir, best remembered as 'Bonnie Prince Charlie' by the Scots, was 'the Young Pretender.'

The pleasantest of this latter group was the Young Pretender's younger brother who became a Cardinal, enjoyed substantial wealth from the King of France, until the French Revolution left him penniless and the much-abused King George IV of England granted him a pension of 4000 pounds a year. He was a charming man and it is told that on one Christmas day, one of his guests at dinner complimented him on serving a real English plum pudding. "Alas," said the Cardinal, who knew the limitations of his Italian chef, "I fear it is only a Pretender."

Relations between the exiled Stuarts and their successors, the House of Hanover, were amiable. The Cardinal bequeathed the Crown Jewels which had been carried off by James II, to King George IV of England, and in 1819 George contributed generously to the erection of the fine monument by Canova, which you may still see in St. Peter's in Rome. It proclaims itself the tomb of James III, Charles III and Henry IX, of England.

There are still people who regard the Stuarts as the true English monarchs. When I was at Oxford (1935-38) there was a quite flourishing White Rose Society in the University, the sole purpose of which was to proclaim and support the pretension of a obscure European prince to that dignity. To find out how the Stolbergs and the Sobieskis come into this complex story (and into my play) you must look in books of reference.

Hunting Stuart may be taken as a play about Canadian snobbery, though I hope that will not be your chief interest in it; after all, snobbery, even at its meanest, is an acknowledgement of something worthy of admiration; if that object is something fine, is the snobbery thereby redeemed? But I intended the play as a reflection on the nature of kingship, and the strong likelihood that royal blood may turn up in unexpected places. There may be an element of nobility in any one of us, and we should be careful not to betray it.

Nor should we be too sure of our opinions. Fred Lewis, the know-it-all young psychologist, discovers that part of the origin of his present-day belief included the discredited quackery of the phrenologist. Not that we should be incredulous about everything, but we should avoid becoming cocksure, especially in matters labelled 'Science,' which tends, at the moment, to discredit the idea of heredity.

Hunting Stuart, by the way, is the name of the dark tartan worn by the Stuarts and their clansmen; it is not the gaudy Royal Stuart, worn on dress occasions. The pun in my title will not go unnoticed. Both tartans are said by some Scots authorities to be nineteenth century inventions, but on such a vexed topic I decline to comment.

The little play, *The Voice of the People,* is a *jeu d'esprit,* not meant to be taken very seriously, but to touch on a human foible familiar to every newspaper man. Indeed, this play has been a favorite with many newspaper people, all of whom are familiar with the subscriber who regards the paper's letter columns as his megaphone and his platform. Newspaper people know that writers of Letters to the Editor, who are unaccustomed to the pen, often need protection against themselves, when indignation has triumphed over common sense.

Robertson Davies

Hunting Stuart

Hunting Stuart

Characters:

Lilian Stuart

Caroline Stuart

Mrs. Clementina Izzard

Henry Benedict Stuart

Fred Lewis

Dr. Homer Shrubsole

Dr. Maria Clementina Sobieska

Cast of the first performance, November 22, 1955,
Crest Theatre Company at the Crest Theatre, Toronto, Ontario:

Lilian Stuart	Frances Tobias
Caroline Stuart	Diane Vandervliss
Mrs. Clementina Izzard	Helene Winston
Henry Benedict Stuart	Donald Davis
Fred Lewis	Eric House
Dr. Homer Shrubsole	Max Helpmann
Dr. Maria Clementina Sobieska	Barbara Chilcott

The scene is the principal room in the apartment of Henry Benedict Stuart, a minor civil servant, in Ottawa, Canada. Our first impression is one of clutter and fussiness of a rather pathetic sort; so much has been done, and done so badly, to make this room home-like and fashionable in the convention of the ladies' magazines. But the room itself resists both the striving toward fashion and the trend toward vulgarity. It is the biggest room on the top floor of an old Victorian mansion; the walls bend inward, following the contours of the roof; there are large windows, curious in shape and too near the floor. It is an undefeated old monster of a room.

It serves the purpose of three rooms. At the rear, on the right of an actor facing the audience, a 'kitchen-area' has been devised by means of a half-partition with a counter top, dividing it from the rest of the room; in front of this pathetic bit of pretence is the 'dining area,' which has a table and chairs of a cheap and pretentious kind. The rest is the 'living-area,' and though it may be littered with little pots of ivy, little ashtrays, little tables with little boxes on them and little trash of every description, there is a decent old sofa, and a bearable chair or two. The door from downstairs is at the actor's right; the door into the rest of the flat is up a few steps and off a platform with a baluster, left.

Here is a challenge, then, for the scene designer. Let him give us a room in which the good old quality of the house is swearing at the cheap decorations of its present occupants. Let him give us a setting which is capable of being hideous, pathetic, and, when occasion demands, noble. When he has read the play he will find out why.

Act One

(When the curtain rises it is a little after five o'clock on a November night; through the windows we can see some of the lights of Ottawa glimmering coldly. **Lilian Stuart** *is laying the table for a light meal; she is a woman in her late thirties, and would be pleasant enough to look at if she did not strain so. But there is not a free or unconstrained thing about her; her hair is tightly done, and her clothes are tight; her mouth and eyes are tight. She wears a tight apron – not a work apron, let it be understood – but the kind of apron which ladies' magazines assure such people as* **Lilian** *may be worn without any suggestion of degradation. She puts out paper napkins; she rustles the bunch of artificial flowers into a new, dry paper 'arrangement.' She is deeply occupied with her thoughts.*

Her thoughts are not pleasant. A copy of a newspaper lies conveniently to her hand, and she picks it up and looks at it with deep concern.

There is nothing farcical about her perturbation; she is in real distress.

*The door from outside opens and her daughter **Caroline** crosses the room without a greeting, disappears for a moment into the bedroom section of the apartment, and comes back without her coat and hat. She is eighteen or nineteen and, like her mother, she has some pretensions to looks; but life has not clamped a vice on her yet.*

***Lilian** raises her head from what she is doing, and indicates the paper. **Caroline** picks it up and immediately sees the cause of the trouble.*

All of this takes some time and should work up the utmost possible expectation in the audience.)

Carol: This is the worst yet.

Lilian: I don't know that I can be expected to go on any longer.

Carol: How do you mean?

Lilian: I'll just have to throw up everything – give up everything. That's all.

Carol: Don't do anything in a hurry.

Lilian: Oh, don't worry. I'm not that kind. I'll stick by the ship. But everything else will have to go.

Carol: Now, Mother, don't go Christian-martyring. It's bad, but I suppose it'll blow over.

Lilian: There is such a thing, Carol, as cumulative effect. There is such a thing as piling the load up and up, until the willing horse can bear no more. I'm not unreasonable. I don't expect my friends to put up with this sort of thing endlessly. I don't expect to hold a place which I've made – God only knows with what struggle and sacrifice – in the face of an impossible situation. I'll just bow out as gracefully as the circumstances permit.

Carol: Which won't be so damned gracefully, all things considered.

Lilian: We shall not make anything any better by strong language.

Carol: Well, it concerns me, too.

Lilian: Please, my dear, let us not begin quarrelling among ourselves. I know what this means to you. But, as I am older, and have a place in the world a little more solid, a little more mature than your own, I think it concerns me rather more.

Carol: Yes, it's pretty hard on your social ambition. But I've been trying to tell you that's all built on a false attitude toward life, anyhow.

Lilian: You've been trying to tell me what Fred Lewis has told you. You'd never have thought of that by yourself. When Fred wears off you'll come to your senses again.

Carol: Now, Mother, there's no use being like that. I'm not going to quarrel.

Lilian: No, because Fred doesn't approve of quarrelling.

Carol: Fred's a psychologist –

Lilian: A final year student of psychology –

Carol: If you like. But he says quarrelling is immature, particularly with somebody of your personality-type.

Lilian: I am not a type. If there is one thing for which I thank God it is my individuality.... What's Fred going to say to this?

Carol: He'll probably be able to explain why she did it, and everything. It's not Fred that'll make my life miserable about it.

Lilian: I wish it were. Oh, I know you think you love him, and all that, but I don't like it. What do you know about him?

Carol: A great deal. He's been explaining himself to me, and me to myself, for the past six months. We're sort of growing together through mutual self-revelation.

Lilian: But you haven't met his family.

Carol: I don't need to. He's told me all about them.

Lilian: Are they nice people?

Carol: They've got a pretty faulty marital adjustment, and now that Fred is almost launched in life it's cracking up. But he's sure they'll stay together rather than face the social disapproval that would follow a divorce in their age-group and culture-level. His father is the best of the two. Fred says he's not a bad old spud.

Lilian: You have not met this – old spud?

Carol: No.

Lilian: Nor Fred's mother?

Carol: No. I suppose I will, some time. But what about it? It's Fred I'm marrying, not his parents.

Lilian: Oh, my dear, that's where you're so wrong. When you marry somebody, you marry his parents, and his aunts and uncles, and a whole tribe of people, some of whom you may never see. But they're all there, just the same. And they're all part of Fred. What they are, he is. There's an old saying: 'When you marry you get an old house over your head.' The person you marry is the outcome of generations of – what? Aren't you interested enough even to take a glance?

Carol: I'm not as interested as you are, Mother, certainly. You're hipped on all that family stuff.

Lilian: You know who my family were –

Carol: Yes.

Lilian: It's a distinguished connection, and I'm very proud of it. All father's and grandfather's generation were in the government service –

Carol: And you married Daddy because he was in the government service.

Lilian: I married your father because I was very young, and he swept me off my feet, and I was deeply in love.

Carol: And you're not in love any more.

Lilian: That is not something I can discuss with you. But I ask you, can love survive this? *(Indicates the newspaper.)*

Carol: That's not Father. That's Aunt Clemmie.

Lilian: Your father's Aunt Clemmie. You see? One gets an old house over one's head. I am anxious that you should not repeat my mistake.

Carol: Mother, I don't like to hear you call your marriage a mistake.

Lilian: My dear, you must forgive me – don't catch me up on every word. Just remember this: whatever happens – and plenty has happened, I can assure you, in the past twenty years – I am loyal to your father. And that's because of my family, which has made me what I am. You know the motto on the family crest: 'Ower Leal' – more than loyal. I want you to marry someone who won't strain your loyalty as mine has been strained.

Carol: Fred and I look at things differently.

Lilian: How could she do it? I ask you, how could anybody do it?

Carol: Well, you'll have a chance to ask her. She'll be here tonight. I'm surprised she isn't here now.

Lilian: What?

Carol: It's the day Daddy gets his cheque. She always comes on paydays to get her bottle.

Lilian: How can she have the face to walk the streets?

Carol: She's probably proud of this, you know.... Did Fred call?

Lilian: I don't know. Yes, I think he did. The phone has been ringing all day. So many club calls. There's a meeting tonight; I won't be able to face it, of course. And a lot of calls for your father.... Carol, does your father ever mention any of his women friends to you?

Carol: Now, Mother, what bee have you got in your bonnet?

Lilian: Dear, I've asked you once already not to catch me up on every word. Of course your father has many women friends. All the wives of the couples we know, for instance. And probably others ... you know, when we were married your father was extremely attractive.

Carol: He still is.

Lilian: Who told you that?

Carol: All the girls I know. They all think he's simply terriff. Middle-aged men haven't usually got that – that Thing, you know.

Lilian: That Thing?

Carol: Well, surely you know, if anybody does.

Lilian: When one is married to a man, one moves beyond — that Thing. It gives place to something finer — deeper — a spiritual creation.

Carol: What Daddy has isn't so much spiritual as — well, sort of — *(She takes a deep and audible breath through her nose;* **Lilian** *is not pleased.)*

Lilian: Indeed? And, if I may ask, has Fred got – *(She too takes a breath.)*

Carol: Oh, no! Fred's pure Brain – what he's got goes on getting more and more marvellous long after passion has died.

Lilian: I see. Of course, I've never spoken to you of this before, but as you seem to be very serious about Fred.... Carol, even now, I sometimes notice your father looks at girls.

Carol: Well, why not? Don't all men?

Lilian: Not all in the same way. Your father is very handsome, of course; sometimes I've thought him too handsome, for the civil service, anyway. Of course I would want him to look distinguished, but not too much so. 'Nothing in excess' is the creed of the gentleman, my father always said. But your father –

Carol: Well, he is really a foreigner, isn't he?

Lilian: No dear, that's just part of a misunderstanding. His family lived abroad for a time; that is all. But Carol, be very careful about Fred. During the early years of our marriage I had some shocks, I can tell you. Finally I had to reach an understanding with your father.

Carol: Well? Go on.

Lilian: It was his sense of humour, or so he called it. There are moments that come in a marriage, dear, that are sacred; either they're utterly sacred or they are utterly intolerable to a refined woman. A husband has to be made to understand that. Sometimes, at a supremely sacred moment, your father would laugh. I couldn't bear that. It made me feel, in the most dreadful way, unmarried.

Carol: Was he ever unfaithful to you?

Lilian: Certainly not! We won't talk about it any more. But tell me, has your father ever mentioned a woman doctor to you?

Carol: No.

Lilian: There have been several calls today from a woman doctor and from a man who seems to be a friend of hers – or something. She wants to get in touch with your father.

Carol: Did she give a name?

Lilian: Yes, but I couldn't understand it very well. She had a foreign accent. The name sounded like Doctor Sobski.

Carol: Well, I hope it's nothing else to make trouble. *(A buzzer sounds.)* Bet that's Aunt Clemmie.

Lilian: Must I see that hateful woman?

Carol: You'll have to eventually. Better get it over now. *(She presses a button which releases the lock downstairs.)*

Lilian: You're not to leave us alone.

Carol: All right.

Lilian: She's not staying to supper under any circumstances.

Carol: Then you'll have to get her out before Daddy comes home.

Lilian: I'll get her out in two minutes.

Carol: She won't want to go without her bottle.

Lilian: She'll go when she hears what I have to say.

Carol: Easy, Mother. Don't say anything you'll regret.

Lilian: There is nothing that I could possibly say to your Aunt Clemmie that I should regret. I've been thinking of things to say to her for twenty years.

The door opens and **Mrs. Clementine Izzard** *comes in; she is a small old lady, and, without being extremely fat, she is stout in a loose, rolling, unpredictable way. Her clothes are numerous and unfashionable; she carries a bundle or two and a dozen fresh newspapers in a roll. Her hat has a pleasant mingling of the late Lady Laurier and a charwoman's. Her hair is never in good order, and she has special trouble with several witch-like wisps. But she has abundant good spirits and a bright and rolling eye. She may have a trace of foreign accent. She greets them with a glad cry.*

Clemmie: Hi, girls! I've got somethin' to tell ya!

Their reception of her could not be colder, but **Clemmie** *regards this as her nephew's house, and beams upon them without malice. She sits in the best chair, her bundle of papers on her knee.*

I'm in the papers again.

Carol: So we saw.

Clemmie: You did? Oh, and I was hoping to surprise you! Still, you don't get into the papers to keep things secret, eh? I brought a copy for you. I've got a dozen here, all to give away.

Lilian: We have our own copy, thank you.

Clemmie: Well, you'll be able to use another, won't you? I know Ben'll want an extra copy or two. *(She extends a paper to* **Carol**.) Here; take ahold. (**Carol** *does not respond.*) Come on; take ahold; I got lots of 'em. Say, what's the matter with you two? You look like something awful had happened.

Lilian: Do you seriously expect us to be pleased about this?

Clemmie: Why not?

Lilian: Why not? Well, if you really mean that I suppose there's no point in discussing the matter. It's what I've always said: there are people you simply can't get through to – they don't speak the same language – it's something that –

Clemmie: Say listen – I speak English just as good as anybody. I was brought up to speak English; we came out from the Old Country before I was fifteen. So don't you throw that up to me about not speakin' the same language because it's a lie.

Carol: That's not what Mother meant.

Clemmie: I know what your mother meant; she meant she don't like me and she never has. Well, I don't give a hoot whether she likes me or not, because I like her. I don't say I like her personally, but I like everybody on principle because that's the right way and the healthy way to live, and so she can sniff and sneer at me and poison herself with hatred all she wants, but I'll go right on sending out rays of universal love. I'm what the Movement calls a Power-House of Positivity. So put that in your pipe and smoke it!

Lilian: You are completely mistaken! I intended no reference whatever to your racial background; if there is one thing I have always stood for it is tolerance and a warm welcome to all our New Canadians, whatever their place of origin. I'm sure the Stolbergs were very fine people –

Clemmie: You're darn right the Stolbergs were fine people –

Lilian: – wherever they may have come from –

Clemmie: Don't forget your husband's a Stolberg –

Lilian: My husband is a Stuart.

Clemmie: That's another branch of the family – way, way distant. He's pure Stolberg, say what you like!

Lilian: This is beside the point. When I said we did not speak the same language I simply meant that our ideas and ideals are so utterly different that we can never hope to understand one another. How you can do a thing like this and be proud of it – ?

Clemmie: What's wrong with it?

Lilian: Can't you realise how this will look to the hundreds of people that know we are related to you? What will my husband's superiors in the Department think of it? You know – you must know – how much a civil servant's promotion depends on his private reputation! And what about my friends? I've tried – God knows how I've tried – to be more than just a dingy little housewife, to play my part in the world of active, thinking, vital women who are spreading their influence everywhere, and making themselves felt in the councils of the nation –

Clemmie: Gas-bags. If there's one thing sillier than a gas-bag in pants it's a gas-bag in skirts.

Lilian: You're talking about something you simply don't understand.

Clemmie: When I was young, women like you tried to make themselves important in society by climbing up through teas and dances and soirées; now you climb up through clubs and executives and committees. But it's just the same climb.

Lilian: I am not obliged to climb. I was brought up in a certain position. And one of the things that position carried with it was a desire, and an obligation, to serve. But how am I to carry on if I am thwarted and set at naught by this sort of thing?

Clemmie: What makes you think you're the only one that wants to do anybody any good? I'm serving too, the best way I know how. It's not for me to say, of course, but I wouldn't be surprised if in the eye of God I'm not serving a hundred or even a thousand times more than you can. I bet if we could ask God this minute –

Lilian: Oh, for Heaven's sake, be quiet! I might have known you'd get around to something like that! Please leave. I really can't bear any more.

Clemmie: I want to see Ben.

Lilian: Not tonight. I must ask you to go at once.

Clemmie: No, I want to see Ben; he's got something for me. Medicine for my bad hand. He never forgets, the dear boy.

Lilian: We'll get your bottle of liquor to you, if that's what you want. Now, Clemmie, you must go.

Clemmie: Are you trying to throw me out?

Lilian: Put it that way if you like. Believe anything you like, but go.

Clemmie: I won't budge. If you're in real trouble, I'll give you one of my semi-silent treatments. Just you sit quiet and I'll positivize in a whisper.

Carol: Now look here, Aunt Clemmie, Mother's very overwrought, and you know why. The least you can do is leave us when she asks you.

Clemmie: No. It gets clearer and clearer. You need me here. I'm a Positive Power-House.

Lilian: I warn you, if you will not go I may do something we shall all be sorry for.

Clemmie: Not me, my conscience is clear. I'm, like they say, insulated against Evil.

Lilian: Oh! – Clemmie, I may strike you.

Clemmie: Go ahead, but I'm going to stay and see Ben. And I love you, whatever you may do. I'm loving you right this minute. I'm beaming love toward you just as hard as I can. I'm positivizing, Lil, right straight at you!

Carol: Mother!

Lilian, *goaded beyond endurance, has seized* **Clemmie** *and tries to pull* *her out of the chair. But the little woman is solid, and, though the struggle tousles her somewhat, she cannot be moved.*

Clemmie: *(her eyes shut and her teeth set)* I love you, do you hear me! I love you! I love you!

Lilian: How dare you, you disgraceful, horrible, hateful old thing! I won't let you say it! Do you hear me! Shut up! Shut up! **Shut up!**

Clemmie: You can't stop me. Love is stronger than hate! Perfect love drives out Evil! I love you, Lilian! I won't shut up. I love you. **I love you!**

Unnoticed, the door opens and **Henry Benedict Stuart** *comes in; he is a dark, handsome man with a close-clipped moustache; there would be an air of distinction about him if he were not so perfectly content to play second fiddle to everyone. Tonight he is in high spirits. He looks in amazement at the scene.*

Stuart: Hi! What's going on? Lil! Clemmie! What are you doing?

Clemmie: Oh, Ben, you dear boy, I knew you'd understand. I just came here to tell you all my news, and –

Stuart: No, Clemmie, my news first. First of all, drinks – big ones for grownups, and a little one for little Kitty. Now then: I've got a promotion in the Department. From now on I'm Number One C.I.P.

Clemmie: Oh, Ben dearie, isn't that wonderful – Number One C.I.P.! I always said you'd get to the top of the tree, whatever some may have thought.

Lilian: As that is obviously meant for me, perhaps you will be good enough to explain what Number One C.I.P. is.

Clemmie: It'd be enough for most women that it was Number One, without a lot of fuss about details. But oh, no – not my lady; **she's** born to the civil service; **her** father was postmaster in Arnprior.

Carol: Clemmie, stop it. What's Number One C.I.P., Daddy?

Stuart: Well, it's a new post, that every Department is having to create. There are so many letters, you see, that can't be answered at once, and so many that shouldn't be answered at once, and so many that should be but nobody can be bothered, that there is a vast amount of correspondence that doesn't really belong to anybody. Everybody has an In-Box, and an Out-Box and a Pending-Box, for letters, right from the Deputy Minister down. My new job is to get everything from everybody's Pending-Box, and mess it about a bit, and send it to different people every day, till something decisive happens to it, or it gets lost, or the original writer forgets, or gives up, or even dies. All the stuff I deal with is called Correspondence in Pendency, and I'm Number One C.I.P. I'm to have a couple of juniors to help me, and there's a good chance that in time it will work up to be a little sub-department within the Department. It will all depend, if you'll forgive the remark.

Clemmie: Do you get more money?

Stuart: Yes, a bit more, but the best thing of all is that I've been upgraded in the service. I know that'll mean a lot to you, Lil. *(But **Lilian** cannot meet his eye, and weeps a little.)* Why, what's the matter?

Carol: Do you think you've upgraded us as much as Clemmie has degraded us?

Stuart: Oh, Clemmie, have you been at it again? After your promise?

Clemmie: Well – I won't try to conceal anything from you, Ben. The fella was just too persuasive for me.

Stuart: Did he give you much?

Clemmie: Oh, Ben, this wasn't one of those one-shot cash deals; I got a contract and a big cheque. And he's coming back every month for a year. He says I'm just exactly what he's been looking for – experienced, and all. How was I to stand out against an offer like that, and me with not much more than my bare Old Age Pension?

Stuart: But Clemmie, you know I'd have helped you; if things are too hard I could find a little more for you – especially now.

Clemmie: I know that, Ben. You've been just like a son. But dearie, how could I ask you? Look at you living in a flat like this in the Old Town, when in your position you ought to be in a semi-detached somewhere in a nice suburb. I know Lil lays that at my door. I don't want to be a burden, honest I don't.

Stuart: You've never been a burden, Clemmie.

Clemmie: Yes I have, and the worst of it is I needn't be, not while I've got this – well, I suppose you could call it a gift. Honest, Ben, I feel I'm meant to do it. Like the fella said, 'You're the type, Mrs. Izzard, you've got that sincerity,' he said. 'You can put your heart into it where others your age wouldn't,' he said. Honest, Ben, I feel called to it.

Stuart: All right, Clemmie, don't upset yourself. Let's have a look at the paper. I suppose it's much like the others?

Carol: No, it isn't. This time it's a quarter-page. And a picture by Karsh.

Clemmie: No, not Karsh, lovie, but a nice young fella that imitates him. *(She hands* **Stuart** *a newspaper, which he opens until he finds what he is looking for, and starts.)*

Stuart: Fish, Clemmie, it's big. *(Reads.)* 'Mrs. Clementine Izzard, 3204 Avenue Israel Tarte, Hull, P.Q., writes: "For years I was a martyr to distress after meals, and suffered agonies of bloating, gas, stabbing pains, hot searing liquids rising in the throat, as well as faulty and incomplete elimination, causing a logy, dragged-down feeling which took away all my zest for life. When I thought I could endure no more, a friend recommended your Flush-of-Youth tonic; I felt better after the first dose and now could not be without it. I want everybody to know that Flush-of-Youth can be theirs, as it is mine." A facsimile of this testimonial, personally signed by Mrs. Izzard, the Flush-of-Youth Lady, is yours for the asking.'

There is a long pause, during which **Stuart** *takes this in;* **Lilian** *and* **Carol** *are in attitudes of angry dejection; he is bereft of speech; but* **Clemmie** *has a further secret, which she can contain no longer.*

Clemmie: I guess I better tell you now. There's talk of television! They might want me to go on five days a week as the Flush-of-Youth Lady, and sing little jingles. Lucky I've still got a pretty clear voice. *(Another pause, while they drink this in.)* Don't you like the picture? 'Gracious' was the word the fella from the advertising agency used; he says that they want to build me up into a kind of a sweet old goddess, giving out good health.

Stuart: You say you have a year's contract for this?

Lilian: Is that all you can find to say? What earthly difference does a contract make?

Stuart: Well – a lot. It makes Clemmie a professional model, or testifier, or whatever you like to call it. It's different from getting a couple of dollars here and five dollars there for writing a letter for one of these patent medicines.

Carol: Will you ever forget them! 'Before I took Reno-Rite I was forced to rise three or four times every night, but now –'

Lilian: No, no; the worst was 'After baby came I was in agonies with nerves, hallucinations and female disorders of every description.' You, that never had chick nor child in your life.

Clemmie: I got a strong psychic streak, and I know if I'd ever had a baby I'd have had all of that. Anyway, that was creative: I was using my imagination to help thousands of poor women who had babies and misery with them.

Lilian: You didn't help this woman, or Carol either. We were made ridiculous. Worse, we all looked shady, because of you. Do you know what you are, Clemmie? You're an impostor, and I hope the Medical Association gets after you!

Clemmie: Lil – you wouldn't put them onto me! Not on your own kin!

Lilian: You are no kin to me! I want that understood. I'm at the end of my tether, Ben, and I'd better say my say now –

Stuart: Wait, Lil. You're over-excited. You exaggerate what people think. After all, how many people know that Clemmie is your aunt – even by marriage?

Lilian: Everybody that matters knows. Every woman at the club knows. Oh, Elsie Gilkinson saw to **that**, you may be sure, away back in the Reno-Rite days. And after that baby came – and you every day of seventy at the time, Clemmie – she seriously proposed that I be dropped from the executive. There are three hundred and eighty-two women at that club, Ben, and every one of them has a pack of friends and a tongue like a two-edged sword.

Stuart: Oh, come on; haven't they any sense of humour?

Lilian: Yes, they have! And what a sense of humour! Tonight I was to have read them my paper on 'Some Local Pioneer Families Connected with the Nobility and Gentry of Great Britain.' Even if I dropped the one trifling reference to my own family, you can imagine how that would sound in the face of this!

Stuart: Oh, Lil –

Lilian: No, Ben, it's useless to talk any more. I'd depended on that paper – that paper that's taken me weeks and months to prepare – to get me on the National Executive. But that's all done, now.

Stuart: Surely not –

Lilian: Surely yes. I won't go. I'll phone and say that I'm ill. My real friends will understand. And as for the others – well, I'll face the music at the next meeting, and resign. And because of you, Clemmie, I won't even be able to say it's because of ill-health. *(She can bear no more of her own self-pity, and she weeps; there must be nothing farcical about it; her distress is real.)*

Stuart: Have some of your drink, Lil. It'll do you good.

Clemmie: Well, I'm sorry to have caused trouble, I'm sure, and if it'll make things any easier, I'll go. But I must say I think all this is kinda silly. I don't see how I come between you, Lil, and the nobility and gentry, just because I'm going to be the Flush-of-Youth Lady. Heaven sakes! The nobility and gentry are always advertising something – face creams, and food and booze – and even socks – and who thinks less of them for it? Of course, they're noble and gentle already, and not just members of your club that wish they were, and maybe that's what makes the difference. But I've signed my contract, and I'm proud to be doing something that's going to bring better health to thousands – maybe millions. I'm a positive force –

Carol: Yes, I know. And everybody at the university is going to tell me that you're a moving force as well. That's what I'll hear, for weeks to come.

Clemmie: Why, Caroline, I'm downright shocked to hear you say a thing like that! It's coarse! When I was a girl nobody would have dreamed of saying a thing like that to a young lady. There are some things that can't be joked about, and a person's elimination is one of them.

Carol: I've heard plenty about what's sacred tonight. I suppose my generation has its crazy ideas, too.

Lilian: Yes, and a lot of them are called psychology.

Clemmie: Now Lil, don't you knock psychology. I'm a great believer in psychology, and the power of positive thinking and love conquering hate and all that. In fact, come to think of it, there's nothing love won't conquer if you give it a chance.

Carol: Well, why don't you put it to work on your gas and faulty elimination, then?

Stuart: Now, Kitty, that's not a proper way to speak to Clemmie.

Carol: I'm tired of speaking to Clemmie in a proper way. I'm sick of her tricks.

Clemmie: You're all ashamed of me, I can see that. But you don't understand and I forgive you. You're just trapped in a negative thought-pattern, and say what you like, I love you. It's no trouble to love you, Ben, but I have to put my mind on it to love your wife and daughter. But that's where it does good, you see – when it's an effort. I've got a strong, strong love for both of you negativizing snobs and nothing you can do will destroy or overcome it. I love you. I love you. I affirm it strongly. I love you.

The buzzer sounds.

Carol: That'll be Fred. *(She pushes the release on the lock, and goes into her bedroom.)*

Clemmie: Well, I must say this isn't much of a celebration. But I've got friends who'll think differently, and I suppose I'd better get along and see them. Did you say you had a parcel for me, Ben?

Stuart: Your payday bottle, Clemmie; lotion for your bad hand. My celebration's been a bit flat, too. Pity we both had a success on the same day. You see, old girl, not everybody looks at these things the same way.

Clemmie: But Ben, I only want to do people good – help 'em, you see. If I can do it by positive thinking and love, fine. If I can do it by Flush-of-Youth, fine. You know what I am, Ben? I was reading about it in a book. I'm what's called an empiricist. It means I'll string along with anything, if it works.

Stuart: Oh, I know, Clemmie, I know. But while you're finding out if a thing works it's sometimes pretty rough on the bystanders.

Clemmie: Aw, Ben, I'd just hate to think I'd made things hard for you. I keep forgetting about Lil being so different from us. Ben – you're not sore at me, are you Ben?

Stuart: No, no, sweetie, not a bit. I just wish sometimes you had a little more worldly wisdom, that's all.

A knock at the door and **Fred Lewis** *enters; he is perhaps twenty-three and has a serious, intent air which he thinks becomes a psychologist and scientific observer of mankind; he is too full of green knowledge at present to have any sense of humour.*

Fred: Hello.

Stuart: Hello. Kitty'll be here in a moment. You know my wife?

Fred: Hello.

Lilian: Good evening, Mr. Lewis.

Stuart: Kitty's great-aunt, Mrs. Izzard.

Fred: Oh, yes? Hello.

Stuart: Are you and Kitty going to a movie?

Fred: No. We were, but in the light of what's happened, we'll go for a drive instead. I've got the family car.

Stuart: In the light of what's happened – ?

Fred: About Mrs. Izzard. We might meet some of our friends and Caroline would feel embarrassment. Unnecessary, but until after we're married I feel I should take some account of these things.

Stuart: Just a minute, Fred. Did I understand you to suggest that there is something embarrassing about Mrs. Izzard?

Fred: Of course. You must have seen the papers. Her picture and name appear in a large advertisement for a laxative. Our society has an ambivalent attitude on the subject of laxatives. It thinks of them with a complex of humour and abhorrence; fear and desire. Caroline understands all that, but still, she is a product of her society and environment, and she isn't completely free of prejudice. That will have to wait until we're married.

Clemmie: Say, you certainly found your tongue, didn't you?

Lilian: What do you mean – 'free of prejudice after you're married'? Who said you were going to be married?

Fred: We seem to be heading that way. And as soon as we're married, we'll both get jobs in the States and be psychoanalysed. That ought to clear the decks for at least five years of satisfactory adjustment. At the end of five years we'll consider.

Stuart: See whether you want to extend the lease for another five years on the same terms?

Fred: If you want to put it that way.

Lilian: And you think I would permit my daughter to marry anyone who has ideas like that?

Fred: Parents have been saying that since the Ice Age. Your daughter is pretty well-adjusted, considering everything. We'll continue to develop, psychologically. Didn't it ever strike you that after five years she might be glad to be rid of me?

Lilian: It strikes me right this minute that she would be a fool if she ever let herself see you again.

Fred: Now, Mrs. Stuart, let's be reasonable. You've been married about twenty years. If you'd had a chance to break it up after five or ten years, wouldn't you have done so? You know you would.

Lilian: How dare you say that!

Fred: Caroline has told me about your difficulties. Let's not pretend to one another.

Lilian: Carol has – !

Fred: What do you suppose courting couples talk about? They spill everything they know about their families. That's one of the main things that throws young people together – the deep-rooted need to beef about their families. And to brag about them too. Caroline has told me about your Scotch pioneer background, and what a lot you make of it. And about Mr. Stuart not getting along as well as you'd hoped, and about your blaming it on his coming from foreign immigrant stock. But don't think I'd blat it around. It's all very human, and even kind of lovable. The human comedy, I guess you'd call it.

Lilian: Ben, aren't you going to do anything about this?

Stuart: I don't think so. There are a lot of ways in which I'm a failure, and one reason for that is that I haven't much indignation.

Lilian: But to be insulted in your own house!

Stuart: Fred doesn't mean to be insulting. After all, **he** didn't say that I was disappointing because my family came from Europe. He just seems to be repeating the party line as he got it from Kitty, who got it from you, my dear.

Lilian: What I say to my daughter in family confidence should be kept in confidence. It's disloyal to talk to a stranger like that. And loyalty is the mainspring of my character! Loyalty to country, to church, to home! 'Ower Leal' has been my family's motto and watchword for a score of generations! 'Ower Leal.'

Stuart: In that case, my dear, you have no reason to reproach yourself. And the least you can do is assume that Caroline is a worthy product of your training.

Fred: You know, that makes sense. You'd have made a good psychologist, Mr. Stuart.

Stuart: God forbid! Psychology seems to be the Quakerism of our day; speak the truth, spare none and respect none. It sounds fine in precept, but it's hellish in practice. I've never been much of a man for Quakerism in any of its forms.

Fred: That's because you were brought up a Catholic.

Lilian: What? What did you say?

Stuart: It's true, Lil. That's something I told Kitty that I don't think I ever told you. Only till I was six. But you know what the Jesuits say: 'Give me a child until he is six and he is mine for life.' Clemmie will tell you.

Clemmie: We sort of relapsed after we came to this country, and Ben was the last one in the Old Faith. When I took Izzard I got onto this business of loving everybody and since then, religiously speaking, I've been on my own.

Lilian: No wonder I could never get you to church. Not even to the Sunday School Fathers' Night.

Stuart: No wonder at all, Lil.

Caroline *comes in from the bedroom; she has changed her clothes and is plainly pleased at the thought of her evening; we see her now as we have not seen her with her family.*

Carol: Sorry to keep you waiting, Fred.

Fred: That's all right. I've been having a frank talk with your folks.

Lilian: Frank is not the word I should have used. It's been devastating! Caroline, I feel that I hardly know you. How could you talk so about your family to an absolute stranger?

Fred: I'm not an absolute stranger to Caroline, don't forget, Mrs. Stuart.

Lilian: In the light of your earlier remarks, that has a decidedly ominous sound.

Carol: Now, Mother, don't work up a lot of nasty suspicions. We're not like that at all. I suppose you're angry because I told Fred something about the family background. Don't you think he has a right to know?

Lilian: What right have you to say that your father is a failure?

Carol: I didn't say that; I said you thought he was. Let's not have a scene about it.

Lilian: You misinterpret me to every Tom, Dick and Harry –

Carol: That's enough, Mother; Fred isn't every Tom, Dick and Harry. He doesn't care about my family any more than I care about his, but he has a right to know. You said yourself, 'When you marry you get an old house over your head.' And you take an old house with you – don't forget that.

Fred: Not that I'd want you to think I take any stock in heredity, because I don't. Environment is important, of course, but heredity doesn't mean a thing.

Lilian: That is stupid, arrogant nonsense, and I hope I live to see you swallow your words.

Stuart: Well now, which blood was it in Kitty that told Fred so much about our family life, Lil? Your good old Scotch pioneer blood, seeping down through all those postmasters, or my queer foreign blood?

Clemmie: It certainly wasn't Stolberg blood, Ben; when we got together with a fella or a girl we never wasted time on tale-bearing. It was the sweet talk and the sparkin' with us, all the time.

The buzzer sounds.

Stuart: Who's that, do you suppose?

Clemmie: Paper boy. This is collection night.

Stuart: (*Presses the lock-release.*) This hasn't been any fun for anybody. Hadn't we better have something to eat? Do you want to have your supper with us, Clemmie?

Clemmie: I haven't been made so welcome that I think I should, Ben, but if you want me I'll stay.

Stuart: Don't take it to heart. Let's forget about the whole thing.

Lilian: That's always your way. Forget! Forget! Everything can be wiped out by forgetting. But I don't forget.

Stuart: Neither do I, Lil. If it will make you feel any better, I'll make a statement, and Fred can hear it if he likes. I seem to have been rather a disappointment. I haven't got on very far in the world. Today's promotion is probably the last I'll ever have, and I admit it's nothing very great. I obstinately insist on sticking by Clemmie, because she's my last living relative, and so far as I'm concerned she can recommend anything at all and it won't make any difference. And in spite of all the reasons I seem to have for being otherwise, I'm happy. Happiness is the one talent I have, and I'm not going to lose it. Now, suppose those of us who have an appetite see what the good fairies have left in the kitchen.

There is a knock at the door, which opens, and in comes **Dr. Homer Shrubsole**; *he is a large, genial man of distinguished manner and expensive dress; he takes in the scene, and at last finds* **Stuart**, *who is in the kitchen area with* **Clemmie** *fetching the supper, which is on plates covered with waxed paper.*

Shrubsole: Have I the honour to address Mr. Henry Benedict Stuart?

Stuart: That's right.

Shrubsole: My card, sir. I am Dr. Homer Shrubsole, and for the moment I shall not identify myself further. But may I ask you a few questions? I assure you that while they may seem rather personal they are not intended as impertinence, and are indeed of the highest – the very highest – importance.

Stuart: Go ahead. You won't mind if I eat something, will you? I'm rather hungry.

Shrubsole: Please don't let me stop you. I presume that these ladies and gentleman are your immediate family?

Stuart: Oh, sorry. My wife. My daughter Caroline.

Shrubsole: Caroline? What a delightfully appropriate name!

Stuart: Aha? My wife's choice. Goes with Stuart. This is Fred Lewis, Kitty's friend. And my aunt, Mrs. Izzard – where have you got to, Clemmie? *(But* **Clemmie** *has disappeared.)*

Shrubsole: I presume that I may go ahead, quite freely?

Stuart: Before you start, is this about Income Tax?

Shrubsole: No, no.

Stuart: Are you from a credit agency, or anything of that sort?

Shrubsole: Oh, quite otherwise, l assure you.

Stuart: Well, if it's insurance, I've got all I can stand now.

Shrubsole: I assure you, sir, it is nothing of that kind at all. It is a very personal matter – of the utmost personal importance.

Lilian: Is it about a will? Has somebody left my husband something?

Shrubsole: You are much nearer the mark, Mrs. Stuart. But if I may be permitted –

Lilian: Of course. Don't let us keep you and Fred, Caroline. Don't be late coming home.

But **Caroline** *and* **Fred** *are all ears and are not to be budged, and, as* **Shrubsole** *speaks,* **Clemmie***'s head appears above the kitchen counter, behind which she is hiding.*

Shrubsole: My colleague, Dr. Maria Clementina Sobieska, and I, have been trying to find you for several months, Mr. Stuart, and it was less than a week ago that we traced you to Ottawa. We arrived here today, and have been trying to reach you by telephone –

Lilian: That was the name! Dr. –

Shrubsole: Sobieska. But you were not at home.

Stuart: *(eating)* You could have got me at the Department.

Shrubsole: That was the last place, sir, that we had any desire to reach you.

Stuart: Why ever not?

Shrubsole: Your Government connection, sir, might have been extremely embarrassing.

Clemmie's *head vanishes again.*

Now, to trouble you as little as possible: is it not a fact that your name, until the age of six, was Stolberg?

Stuart: Yes, it was.

Shrubsole: You were brought up, after the death of your parents, by an aunt, a Miss Maria Clementina Stolberg?

Stuart: Aunt Clemmie. Yes.

Shrubsole: And you assumed the name of Stuart when you went to school?

Stuart: Well, Stolberg had a foreign sound, and there was a story in the family that there had once been an English, or Scottish, branch called Stuart.

Shrubsole: Really? A family tradition? Remarkable. And is Miss Stolberg still living?

Stuart: She was right here until you came in. Perhaps she's gone into the other room. Do you want her?

Shrubsole: Yes, though not so much as we want you, Mr. Stuart. There can be no mistake, I suppose? You are the only living male descendant of Benedict Stuart?

Stuart: My father. Yes, I was his only child.

Shrubsole *goes to the door, taking care not to turn his back on* **Stuart***; he opens it and* **Dr. Maria Clementina Sobieska** *enters; she is a woman of startling magnetism and perhaps also of beauty; she is superbly dressed, with costly furs. She gives an interrogative glance at* **Shrubsole***, who nods his head. Whereupon she approaches* **Stuart** *who has risen, but is still chewing on his cold meat, and makes him a profound curtsy. She then takes his hand and kisses it.*

Dr. Sobieska: Your Majesty!

Curtain

Act Two

The action continues without a break, and, when the curtain rises, **Dr. Sobieska** *is still at the astonished* **Stuart**'*s feet.*

Shrubsole: I must ask you to forgive my wife's rather sudden leap forward in our story. This is an emotional climax for her, as you will understand when we have explained ourselves. Meanwhile – you'd better get up, poppet.

But **Dr. Sobieska**, *with a cry, seizes* **Stuart**'*s hand again and covers it with kisses, then presses it to her heart.*

Yes, yes, I know, poppet, but you are only causing confusion. May I present my wife, Dr. Maria Clementina Sobieska?

Lilian: Dr. Sobski! On the telephone!

Shrubsole: Poppet, you must get up. You are embarrassing Mr. Stuart.

She rises, but continues to fix **Stuart** *with a burning regard.*

Shall I put the matter in a nutshell, Mr. Stuart?

Stuart: I'd be glad if you would. Would you like to sit down?

There is an awkward pause, in which it becomes plain that **Dr. Sobieska** *has no intention of sitting until* **Stuart** *has done so. After some awkward bobbing –*

Shrubsole: You will understand, sir, that my wife and I cannot sit until you do.

This gives offence to **Lilian**, *who is sitting already.* **Caroline** *and* **Fred**, *who are quite unused to etiquette on this level, hover in the background.* **Clemmie**, *whose head has been appearing from time to time over the kitchen counter, pops up again, for a long stare.*

Stuart: That's very kind of you. But I don't understand in the least. I'm obliged to you for your consideration, but is this a game, or something like that? I mean – *(He lifts his hand which, since it was kissed, seems to him to be the size of a ham.)* – I've never been treated like this before.

Dr. Sobieska: My king in exile! Unknown even to himself!

Shrubsole: If you will allow me to explain, poppet – ?

Dr. Sobieska: It's no use, Bibi. My heart is too full. I am utterly unstrung. Pay no attention to me, please. Disregard me, sir, I beg you. *(But she is asking the impossible.)*

Shrubsole: We agreed to be completely scientific, poppet, didn't we?

Dr. Sobieska: But Bibi, I am scientific. This is the pinnacle of my career! Everything, everything, that I have desired and hoped for in my wildest dreams is here, before my eyes – yet so much truer, plainer than I had dared to hope. The proof of my theory – yes, of course, that would have been glorious. But here is so much more! Kingship, majesty, the breathing reality of a thousand years of divine election! *(Once again she casts herself at* **Stuart**'*s feet.)*

Shrubsole: If you don't mind, sir, I think we had better allow her to remain on the floor. She obviously feels happier there. She is ordinarily a woman of coolly scientific demeanour, but you will understand that these are very special circumstances.

Lilian: We don't understand anything at all, and I for one am becoming bored with your wife's antics. You said something about a legacy, didn't you?

Dr. Sobieska: A legacy! A crown!

Shrubsole: We mustn't be extreme, my dear. Not really a crown. Let us be scientific.

Dr. Sobieska: I am being strictly scientific. It is you who accept the sentimentalities and muddles of history. By the most direct descent and strains of blood, the crown is his; that is the reality. The fact that he is not upon his throne is the accident.

Stuart: You'll excuse me if I say that your talk doesn't sound very scientific to me. It sounds crazy. Who are you, and what is all this about?

Shrubsole: Very natural questions, sir. We are research scientists, attached to the Coffin Foundation of New York City. You have heard of it, I suppose? I am not altogether unknown as a biologist. My wife is a distinguished figure in the world of ethnopsychology; we are both, in our respective fields, deeply concerned with the problems of heredity. Not, let me hasten to say, on the trivial level of mice or rabbits or similar research animals, but in the vastly more interesting and significant world of mankind itself. Humanity, sir, is our guinea pig.

Stuart: Am I a guinea pig?

Shrubsole: You, sir – I say this with the profoundest respect – are the Great Guinea Pig.

Lilian: You mentioned something about a legacy. Then your wife rambled off into wild talk about crowns.

Shrubsole: Not as wild as it might seem. You will understand that, in order to study blood strains and inherited traits of mind and body among human beings, it is necessary to do it among those families with the longest, best-authenticated and most fully documented histories – royal families, in short.

Lilian: Royal families?

Shrubsole: But, as you will understand, royal families are extremely reluctant to give the necessary time and facilities to the research workers. I do not think I am betraying any confidence when I say that there is not a crowned head in Europe who has not declined our proposal to live for five years, under hospital conditions, at the headquarters of the Coffin Foundation.

Dr. Sobieska: They were like mules.

Shrubsole: Don't be too hard on them, poppet. My wife is particularly distressed by their attitude because she is, though somewhat remotely, of royal blood herself. The part played by the Sobieski family in European history is undoubtedly familiar to you. Indeed, sir, my wife is a thirty-second cousin of your own.

Stuart: Oh? That's very nice. How do you do, again? But who, precisely, am I?

Shrubsole, *from his briefcase, produces a long and handsomely engrossed scroll, on which not only a family tree, but small coats of arms are drawn.*

Shrubsole: Your family tree, sir, upon which I shall have the great honour to enter your name here.

Stuart: Stuart; Sobieski; Stolberg – here's my father. And here's Clemmie. Clemmie, come out! Where has she got to?

Clemmie *comes from behind the counter, at last, and all but* **Shrubsole** *and* **Dr. Sobieska** *cluster around the scroll.*

Lilian: But this doesn't explain anything. Will you please tell me, without any more evasion – who is my husband?

Dr. Sobieska: The gentleman with whom you have the distinction to live, madam, is the King of Great Britain and Ireland.

Shrubsole: And, in the light of history, we should probably add – of the Commonwealth countries and of the British Empire.

Dr. Sobieska: In short, he is the oldest living direct male descendant of the Royal house of Stuart. And, with all humility, we hope that he will graciously consent to become the permanent, highly endowed guest of the Coffin Foundation of New York. *(a pause)*

Stuart: You know, that's really a lot to expect me to believe, simply because you have shown me this handsome thing.

Shrubsole: *(opening a large brief-case)* We make no such demand; here are copies, and photographs, of all the relevant material. As you see, there is a great deal of it, but if you wish to examine it now I think that in four or five hours we can trace every major step.

Lilian: But his family have always been so obscure!

Dr. Sobieska: Only since 1788; before that it was extremely conspicuous for very nearly a thousand years. And since the death of Charles Edward

Louis Philip Casimir – whom I suppose you insist upon calling Bonnie Prince Charlie – the descent has been uncommonly pure, owing to the family habit of marrying cousins. You, madam, are one of the few alliances which the family contracted outside its own connection in seven generations.

Clemmie: And I was glad of it, even though I never did hit it off with Lil. I was afraid with all that marryin' cousins the family would get kinda funny.

Dr. Sobieska: That is an exploded theory. Intermarriage strengthens the dominant strain, whether it be weak, or, as in this case, uncommonly strong. I don't think I have the pleasure of your acquaintance?

Stuart: My aunt, Mrs. Izzard.

Clemmie: Clemmie Stolberg that was. I guess if Ben's royal, I'm pretty good, too.

Dr. Sobieska: No question about it. *(She makes a court curtsy, which* **Clemmie** *returns with unexpected grace.)*

Clemmie: Glad to meet a cousin, even when it's so distant. And say, you'll laugh when I tell you why I was keepin' out of your way. I thought you must be snoopers from the Medical Association, getting after me about all the work I've done for the patent medicines. I've been a terrible sufferer all my life, of course, one way and another, and if you want me to go to New York, and settle down in that hospital, I've got lots o' time, and I'd be a good subject, because I'm used to co-operating with medical people, so to speak –

Shrubsole: Yes, of course, madam, but if we can just reassure the Chevalier – I beg your pardon, sir, but it slipped out –

Dr. Sobieska: Yes, we would like to know your wishes, sir, as to how we should address you. May I suggest that, at the Coffin Foundation, ever since we discovered that you existed, we have referred to you as the Chevalier.

Shrubsole: It seemed to us to be suitable, yet tactful. We purposely avoided any such ambiguous expression as Pretender, and of course we must leave it to you as to whether we shall address you as Your Majesty. For our part –

Dr. Sobieska: We were anxious to avoid anything that suggested discourtesy toward the Usurper.

Lilian: The Usurper!

Dr. Sobieska: *(sternly)* Madam, we cannot hear a word against that lady, whose refusal to join in our great experiment was couched in the most unexceptionable terms.

Lilian: But – the Usurper!

Clemmie: I guess Lil feels kinda out of it. She's always been the high-flying one of the family till now, you know – two generations of postmasters. And that club of hers – they talk a lot about the Queen, and toast her in ice-water whenever they have a meeting, and all that stuff. It's kind of a hobby with 'em. When you've made a life-long job out of being loyal to somebody you don't know it's pretty rough to find out you've got just as good, or better, right under your nose.

Carol: Wait a minute. Let's not be ridiculous. This whole thing is a fake. Mother, you're not taking it seriously, are you?

Lilian: I don't know what to think, Carol.

Carol: Well – Daddy, are you going to fall for a story like this?

Stuart: I don't know, dear. But this family tree makes perfectly good sense as far back as I can verify it, which isn't more than two or three generations. We must move carefully.

Carol: But, really, use your head, Daddy. Suppose you are the last of the royal Stuarts – what earthly difference does it make?

Lilian: It might make you a princess. Had you thought of that?

Carol: Oh – pooh! I'm certainly nothing of the kind.

Dr. Sobieska: That is not a matter on which your opinion carries any weight. If you were a princess, you would be a princess if you were a thousand times more commonplace than you seem to be. It is your upbringing, not your birth, which is at fault.

Carol: Mother! Are you going to stand for that?

Lilian: I've often told you about the value of nice manners, dear. Now be quiet and let me think.

Fred: I don't want to butt in –

Dr. Sobieska: But you are butting in. Who are you?

Shrubsole: This is Mr. Harris, poppet. A friend of the young lady.

Fred: Lewis is the name. And I'm a psychologist. And I want to know what all this junk is about heredity. That's exploded. It doesn't matter who Mr. Stuart's family is. We all know just exactly what **he** is.

Stuart: That's quite a claim, even for you, Fred.

Fred: Carol's right. If he's the last of the Stuarts – so what?

Shrubsole: The Chevalier has two choices. The first is to do what his ancestors did, and make a bid for his throne.

Fred: And end up where his ancestors did, flat on his fanny.

Shrubsole: That's a matter of conjecture.

Fred: Now look here. Let's talk sense. Where is he going to get six men, let alone an army that could put him on the throne?

Shrubsole: I don't know that I am obliged to answer you, young man, but in a dreadful kind of way you fascinate me. No one spoke or thought of an army. This is the age of law, you know. Right of property has rarely been so strong; it's the whole foundation of our modern structure of punitive taxation. Governments must protect to the full a man's right to what is his own, in order to protect their own exclusive right to take it away from him. The Chevalier would engage in a law-suit in the International Court at the Hague, and if you do not think that there are hundreds of people who would help to pay his expenses, you know even less about the world than I suspect. The White Rose Society of England would be good for a considerable sum. There are many keen Jacobites left in the world. Even if the Chevalier lost his case, the notoricty of it would ensure him of a good livelihood. As a lecturer alone he would make a fortune. In the States he could have his own restaurant – his own TV programme! His nuisance value in any British elections would be worth thousands! The Scottish Nationalists would steal the whole of Westminster Abbey – stone by stone – to build him a castle! Consider the upsetting influence the existence of a Pretender would have on Commonwealth relations! If the Chevalier chooses to make his presence known in that way, he becomes political dynamite!

Stuart: No, no, no! There's nothing I want less than that! I'm not in the least fitted for it. But you realize, of course, that you have destroyed my peace of mind? Suppose what you say is true; how can I go on being Number One C.I.P.? How can I ever look at an envelope with On Her Majesty's Service stamped on it without a pang? A minor civil servant who is Pretender to the Throne; it's unthinkable! It's downright blasphemous!

Dr. Sobieska: But true, Chevalier. True.

Lilian: It doesn't have to be like that at all. I've been thinking about the whole thing, and I'm not sure I've got it right, but I'm on the right track. We'll send all these documents to England, to the Lord Chamberlain or whoever it is, with a letter saying 'Here it is,' and we lay it all loyally at Her Majesty's feet, assuring her that never, never, never, by word or deed, will we make any use of it to embarrass our dear sovereign. So far as we are concerned, it is as though this had never been. Then – well, perhaps then there will be a letter; and we'll make a little trip to England, very modestly; and absolutely without any fanfare we'll be asked to make a little visit – perhaps only to tea or for a weekend at Sandringham – it might even be one of those wonderful Sandringham Christmases! And there'll be a little private talk, and an understanding, and I'm sure – I'm perfectly sure – that there'll be some word of appreciation of our attitude. And perhaps, maybe years afterward, in an Honours List, buried among all those other civil servants so that only we will recognize the significance of it, there might be an O.B.E., and even something for me. I don't know what, of course, but I have the strangest feeling, a kind of premonition, that it might be a Royal Cypher in diamonds, and underneath it, 'Ower Leal.' *(This dream of glory has brought her near to tears.)*

Clemmie: You mean you'd kinda toady up to 'em?

Lilian: Certainly not! I mean that we would do the only honourable and decent and sensible thing. I would face my Monarch as woman to woman – not as, well, I suppose I must say queen-in-exile – and I would say 'We accept the verdict of History.' There is such a thing, Clemmie, as a moral victory, and it would not be unappreciated; of that I am sure. A certain, well, a certain *rapprochement* would certainly come of it. I mean an exchange of cards at Christmas, and that sort of thing. And permission to use something like a crown upside-down on our writing paper.

Clemmie: Oh, you wouldn't keep it absolutely quiet?

Lilian: We couldn't hope to do so. It would certainly leak out.

Clemmie: At your club, for instance.

Lilian: Things get around.

Clemmie: That little crown upside-down's a good notion, Lil. It could give a lot of class, used in just the right place.

Lilian: Clemmie! You wouldn't?

Clemmie: Well, after all, I'm the real thing. I didn't just marry royalty.

Carol: We're none of us the real thing – whatever you mean by that. We're just what we are, and you very well know it.

Dr. Sobieska: I know what you are, and that is why we are here. You know only your environment, and you cling to it. I don't blame you; the courage of youth has very strict limits. But I know your heredity, and a great deal of study has led me to put unbounded faith in that. You are not just yourself, my dear; you are a twig on a tree, and the life of the whole tree, from its root, is your life.

Fred: Now just a minute; as Caroline's friend I can't let that go by. That's old stuff, exploded years ago. Heredity doesn't count for much, any more. Quote me one authority to the contrary.

Shrubsole: I'll quote you two – myself and my wife. You won't have

heard of our work, but in twenty years or so articles in the popular magazines will have given you a good, broad misunderstanding of it.

Fred: That's as much as to say we have to take your word?

Shrubsole: Not if you insist on demonstration.

Fred: These papers and family trees don't amount to anything as proof of
what you claim.

Shrubsole: I don't refer to those. Look! You will admit, I think, that every
man carries his posterity with him; the seed of a thousand generations to
come are in his keeping.

Fred: I suppose so.

Shrubsole: Then why do you balk at believing that a thousand generations
past are present in him also? You said you were a psychologist, I believe.
Do you know any analytical psychology? You have heard of the theory of
a collective racial memory?

Fred: That's pretty much discredited, all that mystical stuff.

Shrubsole: That simply means that you don't understand it, and have
never met anyone who did. But I tell you that not only a racial memory but
an ancestral memory resides deep in the consciousness of every one of us.

Fred: Even supposing that were true, you can't prove it because you can't
get at it.

Shrubsole: Yes, I can.

Fred: Let's see you do it, then.

Shrubsole: May I have the box, poppet? My wife, as you will have
observed, is of a strongly romantic nature, and this little gold snuffbox is
one of her prized family possessions. An ancestress of hers gave it to
Charles Edward Stuart, the Young Pretender. She thought it an appropriate
container for this brown powder which you see inside it. But the powder is
not in the least romantic. It is a simple general anaesthetic which I devised
a few years ago for use in cases where the heart was not strong. I noticed

that it had the property of arousing memories of the patient's past. And in this concentrated form it recalls not simply the personal past – childhood and youth – but the ancestral past. Do you follow me?

Fred: You're crazy.

Shrubsole: You'll believe it by the time it gets into *Reader's Digest.* But if it is necessary to prove the truth of what we have told you tonight, I am prepared to administer it to the Chevalier. What is your wish, sir?

Stuart: I begin to see what you mean about the Great Guinea Pig. Frankly, I'm not by any means convinced of the truth of what you have told me tonight. I wish I knew more history. I don't really know anything about the Stuarts. I thought they died out, or faded out, long ago.

Dr. Sobieska: No, no; there is a well-known descent through the female line, but the Stuarts were men of many loves, and it is through a male line, not very widely acknowledged, that you are born.

Stuart: Very well. But I suppose there are descendants of kings every-where. I'm half inclined to agree with Fred; I'm a minor civil servant in a British Dominion; what does it matter who my ancestors were?

Dr. Sobieska: That is a very modern point of view and not necessarily a right one. It is simply an idea that suits the levelling temper of our time. Your ancestors believed that they ruled not by the sufferance of man, but by the will of God. Modern man has surprising faith in his own will, but he does not care the toss of a button for the will of God.

Stuart: You are a very persuasive talker, Dr. Sobieska, but I am still a civil servant, with a professional mistrust of ideas and of the unknown. If I am the Great Guinea Pig, couldn't I send some Minor Guinea Pig into the past before me, just to see what happens?

Dr. Sobieska: That seems reasonable, don't you think so, Bibi?

Clemmie: Say, look, if you want somebody to take that medicine on trial, I'm just the one you want. I'm used to it, you see? I can take anything. Just you let me get a glass o' water and a spoon, and away we go.

Shrubsole: No, Mrs. Izzard, it must be someone younger and less suggestible than yourself. You are too co-operative to be a good subject; it would be too easy to say that I had hypnotized you.

Clemmie: I don't care what anybody says, Doc, I just want to give it a whirl. Say, you know what? This is just like that Bridie Murphy thing –

Dr. Sobieska: No, no, madam, please do not mention that buffoonery in the same breath with our work.

Clemmie: You don't like it, eh? Well, I'm an empiricist myself. Come on, Doc, be a sport! Let me try?

Shrubsole: No, the Minor Guinea Pig must be one of the young people, and I would prefer Mr. Lewis.

Fred: How do I know what it will do?

Shrubsole: My dear young man, my wife and I are, in spite of the fact that you have never heard of us, two highly-respected people in the world of science. What we propose to do will be done in the presence of four other people, and we give you our word not to touch you or trouble you in any way while the experiment is in progress. As I told you, this is an anaesthetic, easy to take, painless in its action, and without disagreeable after-effects. What have you to fear?

Fred: Who said I was afraid?

Shrubsole: No one.

Fred: Will I be conscious after I've taken it?

Shrubsole: You will be conscious of your surroundings. You will be able to move and speak freely. But your consciousness will be that of one of your ancestors, and you will see through his eyes. Therefore you will interpret what you see in terms of what he knows. You can trust us to help you if any difficulty arises.

Fred: Who will I be?

Shrubsole: How should I know? Who was your great-grandfather?

Fred: I don't know.

Shrubsole: Would you like to find out?

Fred: You're pretty confident, aren't you?

Shrubsole: Completely. And this is not a hit-or-miss dosage, you know. If I give you enough of what I have here to put you in the year 1855, it is as your most direct male ancestor, as he was at that time, that you will think and act until the effect wears off.

Fred: And how long will that be?

Shrubsole: Oh, it might last a couple of hours. But I'll bring you round long before that. You are a Minor Guinea Pig, after all, and we haven't a great deal of time to waste on you.

Fred: Well – I don't know.

Carol: Oh, Fred; after everything you said.

Fred: It's against my principles to encourage anything that looks like quackery. That's all there is to it, Carol. I'd be laughed at if anybody heard I'd gone in for a thing like this.

Carol: Nobody will ever know. I'll guarantee that.

Clemmie: If Fred's got cold feet, my offer still holds.

Fred: I haven't got cold feet – I've got principles!

Clemmie: Same thing, most o' the time.

Carol: Fred, you'll either do this, or we're finished. I want you to do it, very much.

Fred: Now, Carol, you're not thinking this thing through dispassionately.

Carol: I want to know something.

Fred: You've fallen for this hokum and pseudo-science. And I suppose it's up to me to show you that you're wrong. Though it would be far healthier, mentally, for you to reach your conclusions by yourself.

Lilian: You seem to have changed your mind very suddenly, Carol.

Carol: Yes, I have.

Shrubsole: There's your dose. *(He has measured out a small quantity of the powder on a piece of tissue paper.)* Now, you must snuff it very carefully, right nostril first, and then finish it with your left nostril. Easy; don't snuff like a horse, man. Gently. Ah, ah; left nostril now. Good boy. Now just relax, and we'll wait for you.

They all watch **Fred** *intently; he is sitting in a chair, and slowly the rigidity of his body disappears, and he seems to be asleep.*

Carol: What must we do when he comes to?

Shrubsole: Nothing special. Behave as naturally as possible.

Carol: But if he's in 1855 won't everything seem queer to him? Won't we look odd?

Shrubsole: To a remarkable extent we interpret everything we see in the light of what we know. What he will know is the world of 1855, and he will fit us into that framework very comfortably. You'll see.

Fred: You'll see.

Shrubsole: He's away. Just be tactful, please. Don't try to pull him forward toward today. Let him give the lead in everything.

Fred: Thank you, sir, for your eloquent and kindly introduction. *(He opens his eyes, smiles with the confident air of a tent showman, and rises to his feet; he is still very much* **Fred***, but there is a quaintness – a countrified assumption of a grand manner – about his behaviour now.)* What your Mayor has just told you, ladies and gentlemen, is more than sufficient, I know, to establish my bona fides with you. My great mission, which has carried me the length and breadth of our fair land, is known to you. I come to you with the blessing of the great Dr. J.K. Spurzheim himself and with the encouragement of one even dearer to the science of our century – the mighty Professor O.S. Fowler, acknowledged master of present day phrenology. Of the merits of this supreme psychological system I need hardly speak; those who desire to study it for themselves will be given an opportunity later to buy my introductory treatise *The Secrets of the Brain Revealed,* which I propose to make available to you at the utterly ridiculous – the laughably inadequate – sum of twenty-five cents a copy. But in order that you may have ocular and aural demonstration of the unerring accuracy of the phrenological science it is my intention to give a few illustrative readings of the heads of citizens well-known to you, and I shall make my beginning with your efficient and popular Mayor. *(He places himself by* **Stuart** *and begins to feel his head exploratively.)* Aha, yes, as we might have foreseen in a well-loved public figure, the bump of Vitativeness is developed to an uncommon degree, and is complemented here on the other side of the head with a powerfully developed bump of Benevolence. Acuity of judgement is denoted by this prominence above the occiput, and here, where this depression occurs, we might have expected the bump of Destructiveness in a party less devoted to the public welfare; a man toward whom, at every stage of life, the eyes of his fellows will be raised in search of inspiration and wisdom. At any time in history, and in any place, this man would be a leader. A man, indeed, richly dowered by nature to be Mayor of just such a community as this. And now, with your permission, Mr. Mayor, I shall turn to another subject, and I see among you one unknown to me, but marked by an endowment of beauty, modesty and grace rare even in the lovely gals of our native land. *(Moves to* **Caroline** *and begins to feel her head.)* The skull, as the great Spurzheim reminds us, is the relief map of the brain, and the brain is the child of the soul. Beneath this glorious wealth of hair I feel the bumps which denote Reverence, Womanly Tenderness, Wonder, Ideality, Concentrativeness and – I say it with all the awe which such a quality arouses in any man worthy of the name – Amativeness strongly controlled by Modesty. *(His hands, which have been straying over* **Caroline**'*s head, creep down her neck to her shoulders, and seem at any moment about to dive into her bosom.)* O you young men in whose muscles and brains and hearts lies the future of this glorious land, never forget that your deeds are reflected in the bright eyes of the gals of this country, and that your exploits are celebrated in their tender buzzems. It is for them that you conquer the forest and bridge the rushing torrent; for them you plough the field and garner the sheaves of our swelling commerce. These gals – I say it without fear of successful contradiction – are our most precious jewels, and let him whose bump of Philoprogenitiveness is insufficiently balanced by his bump of Manly Reverence beware, lest he rudely strike the dew from one of them and scatter her petals in the furnace of an unhallowed passion! *(He is almost slavering with eloquence and desire.)*

Carol: I can't stand this any longer. *(She breaks away from* **Fred**.) He's a charlatan!

Fred: Maiden, you know not what you say. The science of phrenology – the fruits of the labours of such men as Gall and Spurzheim – and the never-sufficiently-to-be-reverenced Professor O.S. Fowler – are not to be dismissed in such terms. This is psychological science as it has been perfected in our day, and you shall not blaspheme against it!

Carol: It's not science. It's quackery!

Fred: Miss, I cannot brook that word, even from one of your unparalleled loveliness. Phrenology is the greatest gift of science to the study of the mind, approved by doctors, lawyers, and the most progressive preachers everywhere. For twenty-five cents I shall be happy to give you a copy of *The Secrets of the Brain Revealed* in which you may find for yourself proof of what you have assumed to scorn. Read it; read it, I say, and you will find that your bump of Reverence will be perceptively heightened –

Caroline *is in tears.*

Shrubsole: Everybody had enough? I'll attend to him. *(He goes to* **Fred**, *stands behind him, and deftly puts a couple of plugs of rubber into his ears.* **Fred** *falls silent, sits down again and closes his eyes.)* With this type that's the best way to wake them. When they can't hear themselves, they lose their sense of identity.

Carol: It's my own fault, I suppose. I wanted to know what was behind Fred, and now I know. You see, Mother, I was thinking about what you said earlier – about getting an old house over your head when you married, and all that. When you do think of the battalions of ancestors who stand behind every living soul, it's frightening.

Lilian: Don't feel too badly, dear; they probably weren't all tentshow bump-feelers.

Stuart: After all, he was a scientist, according to his lights.

Clemmie: And so's Fred, even if his lights are kinda dim. What I always say is, everybody has to believe something, and if you go in for this fashionable stuff, like science, it's bound to change.

Carol: But I hated the way he touched me!

Shrubsole *has been working gently over* **Fred**, *stroking his temples and occasionally feeling his pulse.*

Shrubsole: He'll be with us in a minute.

Carol: Will he remember?

Shrubsole: I don't think so; if he asks any questions I think it would be kinder not to tell him anything. (**Fred** *sighs and opens his eyes.*) Well, how are you?

Fred: All right.

Shrubsole: Anything you'd like?

Fred: Glass of water. I'll get it. *(He goes to the kitchen, avoiding the eyes of the others.)*

Stuart: Do you advise me to follow you, Fred?

Fred: Suit yourself.

Stuart: You don't feel any ill effect?

Fred: No.

Clemmie: If you're still worried, Ben, I'm ready to try it. You won't get much out of Fred.

Fred: What do you expect? I've been proved wrong. All right. But I have to take a little time to get used to it. *(He sits down with his glass of water at some distance from the others.)*

Clemmie: I'm ready and willing. I can't say better than that.

Stuart: You've proved your point. And I suppose that if I don't do it I'll blame myself all the rest of my life. But I can't say I feel happy about it. Which of my ancestors had you in mind?

Shrubsole: In the ideal conditions of the Coffin Foundation Institute many, many fascinating bypaths could be explored. But – we scientists are as impatient as others, you know. Tonight, Chevalier, we would like to try for the really big prize.

Stuart: Yes?

Dr. Sobieska: You know, of course, whom we mean?

Stuart: I don't really know one Stuart from another. Didn't one of them get his head cut off, or something?

Lilian: Ben, I think they mean Bonnie Prince Charlie.

Dr. Sobieska: Charles Edward Louis Philip Casimir, the Chevalier St. George. The king of the Highland hearts!

Stuart: I don't know a thing about him, you know. Doesn't he advertise a whisky? Fellow in a white wig and a kilt?

Shrubsole: You don't need to know anything about him, Chevalier.

Clemmie: Say, wasn't he some kind of a bad egg? Seems to me I've heard about him and some girl.

Dr. Sobieska: His life was not always easy, and many spiteful things were said of him.

Stuart: I hate to admit it, but I've got terrible cold feet. There's just something – a hunch I have – that I don't want to do it and shouldn't do it. Hate to be disobliging.

Lilian: Ben, you've said it yourself; if you don't do it, you'll always wonder about it. Tonight, for the first time, something really great has come into our lives. Don't reject it.

Stuart: All right, Lil. You're right, of course. Only I wish I didn't have to do it alone.

Clemmie: If you want somebody to go with you, Ben, you know I've only got to be asked.

Lilian: If anyone is to go with him, I should.

Stuart: Lil, would you?

Lilian: Yes – my king.

Stuart: *(Happily, taking her by the hand)* Well, of course, that makes all the difference. It was the possible loneliness that worried me, you know. Give it to me.

Shrubsole: I have brought your dosage very carefully measured out, Chevalier. Here it is; the pink paper for the right nostril, and the blue paper for the left. Gently; it's quite pleasant if you take it gently. Just a little more. Ah – thank you, sir.

Stuart *has taken his dose eagerly and with courage, and now he relaxes happily in his chair.*

Lilian: Have you the dose for me?

Shrubsole: Mrs. Stuart, I did not like to disturb the Chevalier, but what you suggested was quite impossible. We have no reason to suppose that your past and his own ever touched at any point. And so, to subject you to this experiment would only lead to confusion – two people suddenly removed to the later eighteenth century, but separated by thousands of miles and impassable gulfs of social station. It would be quite useless to attempt it.

Clemmie: You mean you tricked 'em?

Carol: He'll be alone?

Lilian: But – you've sent him away from me!

Clemmie: Doc, I wouldn't have believed you'd be so sneaky!

Shrubsole: Please – I have explained that it would be useless –

Lilian: You've let him get away from me!

Dr. Sobieska: Can't you see? If, as we hope, he should find himself short-
ly filled with the spirit of his great ancestor, what would he have to do with
you? Do you think that you and he have been man and wife since the dawn
of time? You flatter yourself, Mrs. Stuart!

Clemmie: But I can go to him! I'm his nearest relative; surely I can go to
him? He'll want somebody. He's not weak, you know, but he's always been
tender in his feelings, and he'll be scared if he comes to and finds he's all
alone!

Shrubsole: He won't find himself alone, I assure you. And if necessary I
will send you to him. Is that enough?

Clemmie: I'll hold you to that.

Carol: I don't believe your promises.

Lilian: You have tricked me despicably – both of you!

Dr. Sobieska: Can't you get it into your head that whatever you might
prove to be in the eighteenth century, it would not be very likely to attract a
prince?

Lilian: I would like you to understand that my family, though certainly not
royal, has never been anything to be ashamed of.

Shrubsole: Unless you want the Chevalier to find himself in the middle of
a brawl, you'd better all be quiet.

Stuart *shows signs of returning consciousness. And from his first words we
are conscious of a great change in him; this is a confident, aristocratic,
charming, wilful and utterly selfish man.*

Stuart: What o'clock is it?

Lilian: About half-past eight, dear.

Stuart: What fool said that? *Mort de ma vie,* what ninny said that? I'll
have no answer but my only answer, d'ye hear? Now: what o'clock is it?

Shrubsole: Past time for the Second Restoration, and half-past eight, Sire. *(to* **Lilian***)* You'd better not speak to him unless he speaks directly to you, and then use your wits.

Stuart: That's how I am to be answered. Fish, how often must I make my wishes known?

Lilian: I'll speak to my husband as I please.

Dr. Sobieska: He's not your husband now. Just keep that in mind.

Lilian: He is. He's pretending. He said 'Fish.' That's a silly word he always uses.

Dr. Sobieska: All the Stuarts said 'Fish.' It's a family Catholic oath. Please be quiet.

Lilian: I tell you he's pretending. He knows who he is well enough. Doesn't he, Fred? You knew all the time, didn't you?

Fred: No.

Lilian: You know you did. You remember everything you said, don't you?

Fred: I tell you I don't remember anything. Let me alone.

Stuart: I hate whisperers! *(His eyes flash open for the first time.)* Though it is my fate to sojourn here with a pack of Scotchmen, Poles, Italians and brandy-nipping English whores I shall at least be treated as a gentleman, if not as a king. Let me hear no more whispering! God's my life, I must have sleep in my eyes, you look so queer! Walkinshaw! Where are you? *(He advances upon* **Lilian***.)* What are you skulking there for, heh? Get me something to drink, my charmer, and be quick about it.

Lilian: What – what would you like – Sire?

Stuart: What would I like? *Nom de Dieu,* what question's that? What do I always like? What would I like? Walkinshaw, the brandy has washed your small brain away!

Lilian: What should I give him?

Shrubsole: What have you got?

Clemmie: Here's my payday bottle, not even opened. Ben always loved a drop o' Scotch. Try it.

Lilian: Why does he call me Walkinshaw?

Shrubsole: She was the Pretender's most faithful friend till death. She was also his mistress.

Lilian: *(greatly pleased)* His mistress? Well, that's not how I would ever have thought of myself. Still, it shows that it's not so ridiculous to suppose I might have appealed to Prince Charlie as you thought. *(Pours out a very small drink in a tumbler.)* What shall we put with this? I haven't a drop of soda in the house.

Carol: There's a Coke in the fridge.

Lilian: Does that seem right to you? Scotch and Coke for Bonnie Prince Charlie?

Shrubsole: If it's the best you have.

Dr. Sobieska: It sounds disgusting.

Stuart: Walkinshaw, I'm waiting!

Lilian: Here is your drink, Sire.

Stuart: *(drinking) Mort de ma vie,* it's poison! The Presbyterians are trying to poison me! *(He spews it out.)* Walkinshaw, have you turned against me?

Lilian: Me? How could you think so? 'Ower Leal – Ower Leal!'

Stuart: 'Ower' what? What's the matter with you, Walkinshaw?

Lilian: Surely the king of the Highland hearts recognises the old old Highland tongue. 'More than loyal,' Sire.

Stuart: I haven't been king of the Highland hearts, or of anything else, for some time, you old fool, and well you should know it. What have you to do with any tongue but the English tongue, you London slut? And don't prate to me of your loyalty; those who parade their loyalty hope to gain by it. Now – what's this filth?

Lilian: Whisky.

Stuart: Ye lie. It's a vile wine, made from turnips and horse-piss. Why would you offer me whisky? You know I hate it.

Lilian: It's all we have, Sire.

Stuart: O Poverty, thy tooth is keen! No wine? Only the raw usquebaugh of the bare-breached North? Well, get me the bottle. Fish, I've lodged in some lousy cribs in my time, but none worse than this. (**Lilian** *has brought him the whisky bottle.*) Now, Walkinshaw, you old blackleg, we'll make a night of it. Get the cards.

Lilian: We haven't any cards.

Stuart: Get the cards, woman.

Dr. Sobieska: *(producing cards)* Here is a little patience deck. Use these.

Carol: He doesn't know how to play cards.

Shrubsole: Wonderful! Now, Mr. Lewis, what have you to say about inherited memory?

Stuart: What money have you, Walkinshaw? I haven't a sou.

Lilian: Just my housekeeping money, Sire.

Stuart: Give it to me. Now – win it back if you can. You deal. And roll up your sleeves. I know you, madam.

Lilian, *much discomposed, begins to deal as for bridge. He eyes her sardonically, then suddenly dashes the cards to the floor.*

Are you possessed, woman? What do I want with ten cards? Pick them up and deal again.

Lilian: I will not.

Stuart: How's this? Do you brave me, Walkinshaw? Have you forgotten the weight of my stick, bitch? Pick up the cards!

Shrubsole: You'd better, I think.

Dr. Sobieska: It is on record that he once gave Walkinshaw fifty beatings in one day.

Lilian: *(picking up the cards, tearfully)* I only meant that a gentleman would pick them up himself, when he threw them down.

Stuart: *(softening)* Yes, wench, a gentleman might, but would a king do it for a subject? And are you not all my subjects, dearest heart? Is not my whole earthly kingdom locked up in your breast, my faithful Tatty? You must bear with my fancies, dear girl, as I must bear with the world's disorder that makes me the wretched pensioner of the man who sits on my throne. Let's drink to German Geordie! *(He pulls her onto his lap, and lifts the bottle to her lips; she drinks a little, with difficulty.)* What's the matter, mouse? Are you longing for your brandy? *(Takes the bottle and has a long pull at it.)*

Lilian: Stop! You'll be ill in the morning.

Stuart: I've been ill every morning for twenty years. *(Drinks again.)* When I was running for my life in '45, I drank this tipple by the hornful in every croft in the Western Isles; for seven months I was never dry or sober. Seven months; that's long enough to make a poor sort of child, Tatty, and it was long enough to make a poor sort of creature out of me. But still I am a king, lass, though a king with but one subject; and that one subject, my sweetest mouse, is worth all the world together.

He has finished the bottle and is now very drunk, but he holds it well, speaks with more than normal clarity, and staggers only a little. The drunkenness is in his wild and rolling eye, and in his raffish smile.

I'll walk abroad now. Put on your bonnet, Walkinshaw, and we'll show ourselves in the fashionable part of the city. With luck we may meet some fools who do not play picquet as well as we do.

Lilian: No, no; you mustn't go out!

Stuart: I will go out. *(He shies the bottle at her head.)*

Lilian: No – see, we have guests. You cannot leave them.

Stuart: I can leave if I choose. What guests? Who's that?

Shrubsole: *(bowing)* I am a physician, Chevalier.

Stuart: A chirurgeon? Have you come to give me a purge? Your face is purge enough, you dog. Get out.

Shrubsole: I am a royal physician, Sire. Attending here upon the Princess Maria Clementina Sobieska.

Dr. Sobieska *curtsies deeply.*

Stuart: My mother was a Sobieska. Are you a cousin of mine?

Dr. Sobieska: I have that honour, Sire.

Stuart: *(all charm now)* I am truly sorry, cousin, to entertain you in so poor a place. *(For the first time, he is conscious of the whole room.)* Come here, child, and kiss your cousin. My daughter, the Duchess d'Albany. (**Carol** *is confused.*) My old nurse, also a Sobieska. (**Clemmie**, *ready for anything, curtsies profoundly.*) Of Mistress Walkinshaw you will have heard from the tongue of scandal; an honest trollop, except at cards, and she has shared my exile without much complaint. *(to* **Fred**) Boy, bring wine.

Fred: There isn't any wine.

Stuart: *(silky)* What is that bottle I see there? *(It is the other whisky bottle.)*

Fred: It's whisky.

Stuart: Bring it.

Sulkily, **Fred** *does so, assisted by* **Carol**, *who brings tumblers.*

Pour, Walkinshaw. Cousin, let us drink to better fortune. I am sorry there is no wine. *(Holds up a glass of whisky.)* This we must look upon as a Pretender – the second in the room. Boy, have we nothing to eat?

Fred: How should I know?

Stuart: The insolence of Italian servants would be intolerable if it were not amusing. I shall prepare food. I am an excellent cook. I have to be. Walkinshaw is English; she spoils everything. I shall prepare an omelet. *(He goes into the kitchen area, and is soon breaking eggs into a bowl.)*

Carol: But he can't cook anything.

Shrubsole: This is beyond my wildest hope. Poppet, we've done it!

Dr. Sobieska: Bibi, it's a dream come true. And isn't it wonderful?

Lilian: No. I'm frightened. Why am I Walkinshaw? Didn't he have a wife?

Shrubsole: He had Walkinshaw much longer.

Carol: He called me Duchess – something.

Dr. Sobieska: Duchess d'Albany; his daughter. He was very fond of her.

Carol: But I don't want to be a Duchess. I hate all this! It's spooky and dishonest and – and wrong. This is Canada. This is now!

Dr. Sobieska: We've no time for that. Perhaps 'now' is a little bigger than you suspect. Perhaps you are somewhat better bred than anyone could guess.

Fred: Don't take that tone with Carol, Doctor Whatever-it-is. I'm going to call the police. You two ought to be locked up.

Shrubsole: Please, Mr. Harris, control yourself. Because this is beyond you –

Fred: You're troublemakers. I'm going to ring the police now.

At which moment the telephone rings, and as **Fred** *is beside it, he answers.*

Yes? Just a minute. Mrs. Stuart, it's for you.

But **Lilian** *is staring before her, and does not hear.*

Dr. Sobieska: Walkinshaw! You are wanted on the telephone.

Lilian: Hello?

(In a daze, she takes the instrument from **Fred.***)*

Phone Voice: Lilian Stuart, where are you?

Lilian: Hello, who is that?

Phone Voice: Lil, you know perfectly well who it is. It's Elsie. Elsie Gilkinson. The girls are all sitting here, waiting for you to give your paper.

Lilian: Paper?

Phone Voice: Lil, are you sick? Your paper on 'Some Canadian Pioneer Families Connected with the Nobility and Gentry of Great Britain.' Do you mean to say you've forgotten? Lil, there are two hundred and fifty of the girls here, and they've waited half an hour –

Lilian *is transfixed by the telephone, trying to sort out her worlds.* **Stuart** *has come in with his bowl of broken eggs; we have seen him, during the preparation of this dish, finish the second bottle of whisky and fling it on the floor. He goes to* **Lilian.**

Stuart: Walkinshaw, whisk the eggs! What the plague is that thing? Am I mad, or do I hear a hobgoblin's squeak coming from it? Give it to me! *(He thrusts the bowl upon* **Lilian** *and listens to the telephone in wonder.)* Is it a toy?

(As he speaks, we hear faintly the voice of Elsie Gilkinson: 'I really think, Lil, that after all your years in the club you'd be the last to forget our regular fortnightly meeting. I guess I don't need to tell you that a lot of the girls associate your failure to appear tonight with that picture of Mrs.

Izzard that was in The Journal tonight. The Journal and The Citizen. Now Lil, this isn't a time for false pride; if you expect to get on the National Executive – and I know you do – that picture isn't going to make it any easier, but you'll lose out for sure if you show the white feather now....' etc.)

By God it's a dwarf! A dwarf in a box! Ahoy there! Dwarfie, can ye sing? Sing 'When the King Enjoys His Own Again'!

Phone Voice: Who's that? Lil, who's that shouting? Who are you?

Stuart: Dwarf, I am Charles Edward Louis Philip Casimir. Who are you?

Phone Voice: This is Mrs. Orville Gilkinson, Regent of the Clara Faucett McGurk Chapter of –

Stuart: *(fending off the distracted* **Lilian**, *and shouting)* He says he's a Regent! The dwarf says he's a Regent! Curse o' God, I'll have your guts for garters! *(He flings the instrument down, and it is heard squawking with dismay.)* Walkinshaw, I leave the omelet to you. Don't burn it.

Lilian: Oh, I'm ruined. Utterly, utterly ruined!

Stuart: You are bragging, you brazen old fish-fag! You were ruined when you were twelve by an oyster-hawker in Yarmouth. By the mercy of God, no woman can be ruined more than once. After that, she's in the public domain. Cousin, come with me. We have business together.

Dr. Sobieska: What business, Sire?

Stuart: What business do you suppose? Come.

Dr. Sobieska: But, Sire, we are strangers.

Stuart: Nay; cousins. Kissing-cousins. *(He kisses her lingeringly.)* Come to my bedchamber. Walkinshaw, are the sheets clean?

Lilian: You can't!

Stuart: I say I can. And who should know better than I?

Lilian: But you mustn't!

Stuart: Yes, I must. My need is imperious!

Carol: Daddy, don't! Don't!

Stuart: Run away and play, child.

Lilian: This will end everything between us!

Stuart: Rubbish.

Lilian: Have I no claim?

Stuart: None! But you'll get your brandy as soon as we're in funds. Now, watch the pan, Walkinshaw, and don't let my omelet burn! And you, madam, will require precisely the time it takes to cook an omelet!

(He whisks **Dr. Sobieska** *into the bedroom as the Curtain falls.)*

Act Three

The action continues without any lapse of time, and when the curtain rises **Lilian** *turns in despair to* **Dr. Shrubsole**.

Lilian: What shall I do? What shall I do?

Shrubsole: Why not get on with the omelet?

Lilian: Get on with – ! At such a moment!

Shrubsole: In times of stress a little work with the hands is very calming.

Lilian: This is the one unforgivable thing! Another woman, and under my own roof!

Shrubsole: Another man, too, of course.

Lilian: What do you mean?

Shrubsole: Literally, your husband is not himself.

Lilian: Rubbish!

Shrubsole: I warn you. The Chevalier told you to make an omelet. If it isn't ready when he comes back, he may beat you – Mistress Walkinshaw.

Lilian: Don't call me by that name.

Shrubsole: But that is how he regards you. I give you warning.

Clemmie: He's right, Lil. You oughtn't to risk a beating. That one's got the old Stolberg temper, whoever he is. Tell you what, I'll do it for you. You take a nice rest.

She goes to the kitchen and busies herself with the pan and eggs, but the subsequent doings are of such interest to her that she is still very much in the scene.

Lilian: Rest! Only you, Clemmie, could think of rest at a time like this. I'm going into that room.

Shrubsole: Don't be foolish.

Lilian: Before his own daughter! It's vile. It's utterly unthinkable!

Fred: Let's hold on to sanity. Nothing is unthinkable. Monogamy is just a convention, after all.

Carol: Fred, will you kindly shut up.

Fred: Caroline, we're the youngest people here; it's our job to keep our heads and not give way to emotionalism. This kind of thing goes on all the time.

Carol: Not in the civil service it doesn't. Now shut up.

Fred: Oh, all right, if you insist on being naive.

Lilian: I'm going into that room – alone, if need be. But I would think that you would want to go with me, Dr. Shrubsole. After all, that woman is your wife – or so you have led us to believe.

Shrubsole: Dr. Sobieska is certainly my wife, and also my valued colleague in research. What is more to the point at the moment, she is the finest female exponent of unarmed combat ever to come out of Europe; she trained three Resistance movements single-handed. Nothing whatever will happen which she does not choose to permit.

Lilian: That might cover a lot of ground.

Shrubsole: You are unkind, but I take into account your overwrought condition. I trust my wife implicitly.

Lilian: You mean that nothing is happening in that room now which could not go on right here before our eyes?

Shrubsole: That might be extreme. But I am sure that the experiment is under scientific control.

Lilian: Do you love your wife?

Shrubsole: Very much.

Lilian: And you can sit there, utterly unmoved?

Shrubsole: Not utterly unmoved. But I am a scientist – a biologist – and I suppose I look upon the sexual act scientifically rather than emotionally. The world would be a quieter place if more people followed my example. Be reasonable, madam: how many women are there, do you suppose, who have the opportunity of meeting Bonnie Prince Charlie under the circumstances in which my wife finds herself at this moment? Would you ask me to intrude jealously upon a unique experience? If it is decreed that I must be a cuckold, I am well pleased that my horns should be given me by a man who died, for all official purposes, in 1788. It lends a certain distinction to what is usually an ignominious role.

Lilian: And what about me?

Shrubsole: Science has its martyrs, Mrs. Stuart. You may be sure that when the full report of this remarkable experiment is written, you will get an appreciative footnote.

Carol: Listen! Do you hear that?

Lilian: What?

They all listen, and from the bedroom comes the sound of **Stuart***'s laughter, not loud, but merry.*

Carol: He's laughing. Well, it must be all right, then.

Fred: Why?

Carol: Well – if it was anything, you know, like what Mother is worrying about – they wouldn't be laughing, would they?

Shrubsole *and* **Lilian** *are not so sure, and their faces are a study.* **Fred,** *after a pause, speaks to* **Carol** *very gently.*

Fred: You can't count on that, Carol. Some people are very frivolous.... Do I smell something burning?

Clemmie: The omelet! *(She rushes to the pan, but the omelet is a smoking wreck, which, after a great deal of scraping and rubbing, she puts into the garbage pail, speaking meanwhile.)* I'll have to make another. They'll be here any minute now – he said how long he'd be, remember? – and I guess it'd better be ready or we'll see the fur fly.

Lilian: Oh, Clemmie, how could you be so stupid! You were listening to what was being said, instead of watching your work.

Clemmie: Listen, Lil, Ben's my nephew, and if he's a Prince, what does that make me? Not your bottle-washer, anyhow. I said I'd make the omelet, because it's my nature to be helpful to all who are in distress – and that means you. But I'm not **obliged** to be helpful, see? Not that I don't love you, Lil; I love you just as I love every living thing that walks, flies or crawls. But when I'm doing you a favour I'd appreciate it if you wouldn't treat me like dirt. See?

Lilian: I'm sorry, Clemmie. It's just that I'm so distracted I don't know what I'm saying.

Clemmie: I know, dearie. Let's the both of us rise above the whole thing. Positivize, Lil; that's my advice to you – positivize. *(She returns to her kitchen work.)*

Lilian: Well, Dr. Shrubsole, you've succeeded. Science has triumphed. You've kept me here, haggling and arguing, until my marriage has been brought down in ruins, and my peace of mind destroyed forever.

Shrubsole: How can you tell until you have all the facts? Have you no spirit of scientific investigation in you at all?

Lilian: Yes, and I am going to investigate that room right now!

Clemmie: Lil, there isn't another egg in the house! What are we going to do?

Lilian: As if that were important!

Shrubsole: It's very important.

Lilian: I don't care if he never eats again!

Shrubsole: Dramatic, but unrealistic. Is there a corner store where we can get some eggs quickly?

Carol: Not nearby. But there's a drugstore that might let us have a few. Fred could go.

Shrubsole: Much better if you both go. Be as quick as you can. The man who comes out of that room may be like a lion.

Fred: Shall I get a dozen? I suppose Dr. Sobieska will want something, won't she?

Lilian: Dr. Sobieska has had something! She has had my peace of mind! She has had the security and sanctity of my home!

Carol: Oh, Mother, don't go on like that. It's silly.

Lilian: Carol, I forgive you for that because you cannot possibly understand this situation.

Carol: I understand it a lot better than you do. All you seem to care about is that Daddy may be in bed with a woman, and it isn't you. Can't you understand the really frightening thing is that it isn't Daddy, and that he may never be Daddy again?

Shrubsole: Your daughter has a very strong point, there.

Lilian: You said that when he came out from under the influence of this drug he would remember nothing of what had happened.

Shrubsole: That is sometimes the case.

Lilian: That isn't what you said.

Shrubsole: I hadn't time for detail. Scientific matters of great complexity cannot be reduced to plain yeses and nos for laymen.

Lilian: Fred – tell me honestly – do you remember what you were and what you did after you had taken that drug?

Fred: *(with obvious effort)* Yes, I do. Come on, Carol; we've got to get those eggs. *(They go.)*

Lilian: Oh, this is cruel! Monstrous! How do you suppose my husband will ever be able to face me again?

Shrubsole: Why not?

Lilian: Fred has let the cat out of the bag. He will remember. He will know what he has been – what he has done!

Shrubsole: Really, Mrs. Stuart, you have quite the most romantic temperament I have ever met with. He'll remember something of a remote ancestral past, for which he cannot honestly be held accountable. I keep telling you – he is not himself. Try to stick to the facts.

Lilian: What facts? What do you suppose is going on in that room at this moment? Can you possibly have any doubt? I'm not a fool, Dr. Shrubsole –

She is interrupted by a crash and a masculine shout from the bedroom. After the briefest of pauses, **Dr. Sobieska** *comes out onto the landing, perfectly composed.*

Dr. Sobieska: The Chevalier has had a trifling mishap. May we have a small towel and a bowl of icc?

Lilian: You've hurt him!

Dr. Sobieska: I never hurt anyone except on purpose. He has a slight contusion. A trifle.

Lilian: I must go to him.

Dr. Sobieska: I advise against it. Much better if Madame goes. *(She indicates* **Clemmie***, who is well pleased to be so addressed.)*

Clemmie: Ice and a towel. Sure; right away.

From the bedroom comes a groan, and then a cry of 'Hell and Death!'

Lilian: Don't you dare try to stop me! *(She brushes past* **Dr. Sobieska***, who has come down the stairs, and rushes into the bedroom.)*

Dr. Sobieska: Well, Bibi, in such encounters as this things seem not to have changed very much since the eighteenth century. If we ever get that man to the Coffin Foundation Institute, he must have strong male attendants.

Shrubsole: You're perfectly all right?

Dr. Sobieska: Oh, perfectly.

Shrubsole: The great Stuart charm? What was it like? I speak scientifically, of course.

Dr. Sobieska: It takes two to make charm. Have you the ice, madam?

Clemmie: Just going with it now. *(She hurries to the bedroom.)*

Shrubsole: His wife has been giving me the devil. She seems to own him, body and soul. We shall have to be very clever, poppet.

Dr. Sobieska: You must be clever for both of us. I am tired and hungry. What about that omelet?

Shrubsole: Had to be postponed. You were longer than we expected.

Dr. Sobieska: Bibi, you have no unworthy suspicions?

Shrubsole: I have been as objective as possible under unusually trying circumstances.

Dr. Sobieska: My poor darling!

From the bedroom a sound of a chair being knocked over, and a shout, 'Get out, Walkinshaw!' **Lilian** *rushes out of the bedroom in terror, and is soon followed by* **Stuart**, *who now wears a dressing-gown and a scarf around his throat. Wrapped about his head is another gaily coloured scarf, which covers one eye, and the cold towel which has been applied to it.* **Clemmie** *follows.*

Stuart: A pox on all nurses, leeches, apothecaries, quacks and corpse-washers. I have hit my head on a bedpost and you souse me with cold water like a blind kitten. I'll throw you in a pond, Walkinshaw, and see how you like it. Where's my omelet?

Shrubsole: The omelet which was cooked was utterly unworthy of you, Sire, and I have sent for more eggs.

Stuart: And what am I to do meanwhile? Suck my paws for nourishment, like a Russian bear in the dead of winter? Who spoiled my omelet? You, Walkinshaw?

Clemmie: No, leave her alone. It was me; I burned it.

Stuart: You? I forget who you are. This accursed rap on the pate has addled my wits.

Clemmie: I'm a Stolberg, like yourself.

Stuart: Then that explains it. The Stolbergs have been famous for the worst food in Europe since the Fall of Constantinople. They're viler cooks than the English. *Mort de ma vie,* to taste French cooking again!

Shrubsole: An omelet in the finest French fashion shall be prepared as soon as the eggs come, Sire. I promise it.

Stuart: You're a cook as well as a chirurgeon, are you, quack?

Shrubsole: A good cook is the best doctor, Sire.

Stuart: By God, you're right. A witty dog, this doctor of yours, cousin. But I'm hungry! I could eat my own boots, and pick my teeth with the nails. What am I to do till the eggs come? Get me some wine.

Shrubsole: *(to* **Lilian***)* Wine. Quickly.

Lilian: We have no wine.

Dr. Sobieska: Can't you get some?

Lilian: Of course not. If you want wine for him, get it yourself.

Dr. Sobieska: You are extremely non-cooperative.

Lilian: I'm surprised you brought none with you. You seem to have remembered everything else he'd like.

Dr. Sobieska: I have no time to resent your remark adequately, madam, but –

Stuart: Wine! How often must I speak? Walkinshaw, have you nothing hidden away? Hey, not in your bandboxes, doxy? Bring out your secret hoard! Bring it out, wench, or you know what I shall do.

Lilian: Ben, stop this nonsense immediately. I've had enough of it. Come to your senses and tell these people to go! Do you hear me, Ben?

Stuart: I hear you, Walkinshaw, and what I hear displeases me vastly. Why do you call me Ben, pray?

Lilian: I've always called you Ben. Don't pretend not to know your own name.

Stuart: My name, madam, is Charles Edward Louis Philip Casimir, called Chevalier St. George, but by Divine Right King of England and all its possessions. Because you are familiar and useful to me, you may call me 'Sire.' Do so.

Lilian: I'll do nothing of the sort.

Stuart: *(moving slowly toward her)* Do so, I say.

Lilian: I won't. It's no good going on like that, Ben. I know everything. It's all a trick. Fred told me. He remembered everything while he was pretending to be lost in the past. You can snap out of it if you choose – *(During this* **Stuart** *has slowly pursued her around the room and now he seizes her and quickly swings her up onto the table, where she stands.)* Ben, let me down at once!

Stuart: Walkinshaw, you know me to be a man of my word. You see this knife? *(He holds up the bread knife.)* If you do not drop me a deep reverence and call me 'Your Majesty' at once, I shall cut my throat, and you, madam, will have slain your Sovereign. The blood of the Lord's anointed will be on your head and you will be infamous as long as mankind lasts as Walkinshaw the Regicide. Do I hear you speak?

Shrubsole: For God's sake – !

Clemmie: Oh, Lil, hurry up!

Lilian: I won't be bullied! I won't!

Stuart: So be it. *(He flourishes the knife.* **Lilian**, *with a struggle, succumbs, and drops a deep curtsy – not a very good one.)* Aha! And what do you say?

Lilian: *(very low)* Your Majesty. *(She jumps from the table, sobbing.* **Clemmie** *gets the knife from* **Stuart**.) Oh, it's humiliating – humiliating.

Dr. Sobieska: Why?

Lilian: It's ridiculous. He's not a king. He's **not**! He's my husband.

Shrubsole: Every man is a king at some time. And if nobody will acknowledge it, he dies – whether he cuts his throat or by a long, slow withering through the years. It is supremely important to secure and cherish the moment of kingship. Be generous, Mrs. Stuart.

Lilian: You've beaten me!

Shrubsole: Don't say that. Now, while we are waiting for the eggs, can we talk reasonably for a few minutes –

Lilian: What reason can there be in such a situation as this?

Dr. Sobieska: Give her a pill, Bibi, and quiet her.

Lilian: No! I'll take no pill of yours! How can I know what you will do to me?

Shrubsole: May we have your permission to sit down, Sire? There is something we must talk about.

Stuart, *who has been moody since the incident with the knife, glares at him balefully, but walks to the best chair and seats himself; he nods to the others, who also sit.* **Clemmie** *takes charge of* **Lilian**, *who is sobbing.*

You have complained of the conditions under which you live here, Sire; Madame Sobieska and I have come to offer a change which will be a great improvement.

Dr. Sobieska: Bibi, this is premature – this is not the time! What are you doing?

Shrubsole: Leave this to me, Maria. I want to find out something.... May we speak to you, Sire, about what is in our minds?

Stuart: You may speak to me about the Second Restoration. Is it your proposal to recover my throne for me?

Shrubsole: That is not in our power, Sire. But we can offer you a palace.

Stuart: Who pays for the palace?

Shrubsole: Money will be forthcoming for the palace.

Stuart: Where is this palace?

Shrubsole: In the New World, Sire; in America.

Stuart: Ah, you want me to accept the throne of America? Are you trying to make a fool of me, master doctor?

Shrubsole: By no means, Sire.

Stuart: The King of France has told me that he wants to be rid of America. He says it is worthless. Do you suggest that I should go there and sit on a fallen tree with a crown of feathers on my head, and rule over a wilderness of snow and ice? This palace of which you speak would be a tent of skins, eh? Doctor, I spent the most uncomfortable year of my life in Scotland where I went in search of a throne; no more wilderness for me.

Shrubsole: I assure you, Sire, the palace is a reality, and the finest you have ever seen. You shall live there, without a care in the world, surrounded by agreeable company –

Stuart: What kind of agreeable company?

Shrubsole: Men of science, for the most part.

Stuart: Men of science are not agreeable company; they are meddlesome drudges. Now hark ye to me, master doctor; if you want me to go to your outlandish palace, there must be women in it – beautiful women, of every colour and habit; and there must be drink in it – the wines of France and Italy; and there must be food of the best and all that makes life sweet and dear. For I smell your scheme, sir; you think to deceive me, but I have spied your sneaking diplomatic look. This is a bargain of some sort, and you want me to do something for you: I understand bargains, for I have made a few of 'em myself. My price for anything I do will be very, very high, for when you bargain with me, sir, you bargain – humbly be it said – with God Himself.

Lilian: Oh, he's mad! He's mad! You have driven him out of his mind!

Dr. Sobieska: Quiet! Listen!

Shrubsole: You cling, then, to the doctrine of the Divine Right of Kings, Sire?

Stuart: I do not cling to it; I exemplify it. Have I not the Touch?

Dr. Sobieska: Bibi – the Royal Touch –

Shrubsole: Fantastic!

Stuart: No; not fantastic. It is one of the signs that God has given by which his anointed ones may be known.

The buzzer is heard; **Clemmie** *goes to release the lock.*

Clemmie: It's them – with the eggs. Don't stop talking; go on.

Lilian: Thank God they have come. Perhaps food will bring him to himself.

Clemmie: Aw, don't be such a crab, Lil. He's more fun like this.

Lilian: Fun! You call this horrible madness fun?

Clemmie: Well, I never thought life was as simple as you did, Lil. I always knew there was a lot behind everybody, if we could just get at it. And here we are, see? All of a sudden life stops being gray and messy, and gets bright-coloured and exciting. Now, I want you to promise, Doc – me next on that powder. I just can't hardly wait. This makes all that space travel talk look stupid. Doc, do you think you could whip me right back to Bible times? I've always thought if I'd been around to explain things, and soothe a few people down, the New Testament mighta had a happy ending.

Fred *and* **Carol** *burst in with parcels; they are taken aback to see* **Stuart** *in the room, and creep behind him to the kitchen; but he turns suddenly and surprises them.*

Stuart: Why are you creeping there? I have a royal distaste for allowing anybody to stand behind me – it has too often proved unhealthy. Come here. What have you there?

Fred: We brought the eggs.

Stuart: I remember; you are the impudent Italian serving-lad.

Fred: I am not! I've been half over the town for these eggs –

Clemmie: Fred – ssh! Just play along with him.

Stuart: Make haste with my omelet.

Fred: Okay. Right away – Your Highness.

Carol: *(She is in the kitchen area, and she now lifts up the pan.)* Somebody left this pan on the light. It's red-hot.

Fred: Put it in cold water.

Carol: Is that safe?

Stuart: You will ruin the pan, and my supper, you clods. Give it to me. Now, an omelet pan is a delicate instrument and must be handled gently. I will cool it myself. *(He holds the pan at arm's length and waves it gently in circles.)* Let me see the eggs. *(He feels them.)* These eggs are unnaturally cold.

Fred: Sure. Right out of the fridge.

Stuart: Cold eggs must not be put in a hot pan. Bring them up to the heat of the room.

Fred: How am I expected to do that?

Stuart: Sit on them, if you must. But if you break one of them, I shall geld you with a rusty knife.

Carol: Don't be pouty, Fred.

Fred: Pouty? Who ran all over the place to get these eggs, I'd like to know?

Carol: You did, sweetie, and I'll make it all up to you tomorrow. But tonight, just be a good boy, will you? *(to* **Shrubsole***)* Fred's been marvellous; he even got a bottle of wine!

Shrubsole: Fred, I have misjudged you. There is something golden in you after all. Where is it?

Fred: *(producing it from his pocket)* I happened to know the dispenser at the drug-store and he let me have it as a special favour. It's something they use for mixing tonics. What they call a binder.

Shrubsole: *(reading the label)* 'Made from British Columbia Loganberries.' Ah well, we mustn't ask for miracles. Wrap it in a napkin and serve it at a temperature just above freezing. After two bottles of Scotch his palate will be a little dulled.

Stuart: *(who has been testing the pan against his cheek)* I shall prepare the omelet myself. Break the eggs, child.

Carol: How many, Daddy – I mean Sire?

Stuart: All of them. I am hungry.

Lilian: This is ridiculous. I told you – he can't cook anything.

Dr. Sobieska: But Prince Charles Edward was a gifted cook. So we shall see what we shall see.

Lilian: We shall see him make a mud-pie with a dozen eggs.

Dr. Sobieska: Madam, I pity your lack of faith.

Stuart: Now, child, beat the eggs evenly with a fork – a silver fork, not that old bit of iron wire. An egg is the most exquisite, the most delicate thing to enter a kitchen; but if it is not treated with respect, it will revenge itself most horribly upon its tormentor. You must beat rapidly, but not in a fury, and you must beat in a strict rhythm – in the rhythm of a gavotte. **One**-two, **one**-two, **one**-two – *(As he counts, he takes a few dancing steps, in a manner which utterly amazes* **Lilian**.*)* Is the butter ready? *(He tastes it.)* Salted! Impossible. Salted butter is death to omelets. Is this positively all you have? *(He puts the required amount – several spoonfuls for a large omelet – into the bowl, without permitting* **Carol** *to relax in her beating for a moment; indeed, he compels her to dance with him, in order to keep the rhythm steady. They dance round the room.)*

Shrubsole: Get the table ready, Fred. Poppet, you'd better help him; I don't suppose he knows how to do it.

Fred: Nobody seems to think I know anything.

Shrubsole: Well, can you lay a table?

Fred: I've been a waiter at a summer hotel.

Shrubsole: That means nothing.

Clemmie: I'll do it, Fred. You got the wine. That was real good of you.

Stuart: Now we shall add the salt.

Clemmie: *(handing it)* Sure thing – Your Highness. And the pepper, too?

Stuart: No! No! No pepper yet! Blood and wounds! If you cook pepper it turns rancid and ruins your omelet; pepper is added just before serving. Everybody knows that. Everybody but a Stolberg! Now – the pan is ready. *(He pours the mixture into it, and puts it very carefully on the stove.)* Silence – let there be no interruptions while it is cooking. *(He hovers over the pan, occasionally testing the omelet with a fork.)*

Lilian: I don't suppose you have any idea how cruel you are being.

Dr. Sobieska: Cruel? To you?

Lilian: To me, certainly. But more so to my husband.

Dr. Sobieska: I do not understand you at all. We have awakened him to the greatness that is within him.

Lilian: What greatness? Suppose he really is a descendant of the royal Stuarts? What of it? That is long past.

Dr. Sobieska: If I may say so, that is a very commonplace attitude. To know that we have roots in greatness – you call that nothing?

Clemmie: That's funny talk for you, Lil – you that's always been crazy about ancestors. Why, if these people hadn't come here tonight you'd be standing in front of your Club at this very minute blowing about your own ancestors.

Lilian: There is a difference between decent pride, and these ridiculous delusions of grandeur.

Dr. Sobieska: I understand; it is humiliating to have ancestors who would not wish to acknowledge one. Yes, I can see that, Mrs. Stuart.

Lilian: Even supposing it were true – which I am not ready for one instant to admit – can't you see how upsetting and unsettling this sort of illusion must be for a man in my husband's position?

Shrubsole: That brings us to the important point, Mrs. Stuart. What is his future position going to be?

Lilian: What can it be? If he recovers his senses, what can he be except what he has always been?

Shrubsole: That's what we have come here to discuss. You will not, I take it, make a bid for the Crown which the Usurper wears with so much grace, and, I may say, inherited experience?

Lilian: Don't be blasphemous!

Shrubsole: No? Very wise. But, madam, the arms of the Coffin Foundation are outstretched in greeting. We are prepared to offer a very substantial sum for five years of your husband's time, with the option of renewal when the contract is up. You heard me offer him a palace in the New World. The foundation headquarters is a handsome building, near New York, set in extremely beautiful academic surroundings.

Clemmie: What's he have to do?

Lilian: The Great Guinea Pig! He'd be an experimental subject! It's monstrous!

Shrubsole: He would be treated with the uttermost tenderness and care. You would no doubt be able to visit him from time to time.

Lilian: You mean I wouldn't live with him?

Shrubsole: That would be inadvisable.

Dr. Sobieska: Let us be frank – quite impossible.

Shrubsole: But, of course, you would benefit from the great improvement in his income. And – I dislike touching on this because it is an aspect of my country's civilization which I deplore – you would very quickly acquire an income of your own, from magazine articles, interviews and lectures.

Dr. Sobieska: 'I Housekept for History' – that sort of thing. You'd command fabulous rates per word.

Clemmie: Lil, it's a gold-mine! 'The Woman Who Slept With a Dynasty' you'd be called, and nobody could say a peep against it – not even the Legion of Decency. Because you've always been faithful, and didn't know what you were doing, and all that. You know – spicy, but a hundred per cent legal. She's got a fortune just waiting to be picked up, hasn't she, Doc?

Shrubsole: Reluctantly, I must agree that she has.

Stuart *comes forward, carrying the omelet pan very carefully. During the foregoing,* **Carol** *and* **Fred** *have laid the small table and have been hovering near him, seeking to be helpful.*

Stuart: Walkinshaw, you may serve the omelet.

Lilian *bursts into tears.* **Shrubsole** *steps into the breach; he takes the pan with a low bow, and lays a napkin across his arm.*

Shrubsole: The Chevalier shall be served immediately.

Stuart: Cousin, you shall eat with me.

Dr. Sobieska *follows him to the table. At a gesture from* **Shrubsole**, **Fred** *holds a chair for* **Stuart**, *after which* **Dr. Sobieska** *seats herself.* **Shrubsole** *presents the omelet for* **Stuart**'*s inspection, then deftly serves it with two spoons.*

My talents are not many, cousin, and the greatest of them you would not permit me to demonstrate to the full when the occasion served. However, I think that I may claim some skill in cooking. *(He removes the scarf from his head, and the cold compress; the first dawnings of a black eye give him a raffish but dashing and attractive appearance.)*

Shrubsole: Wine, Sire?

He places a glass, and pours a few drops into it; **Stuart** *rolls it thoughtfully over his tongue, and seems almost to chew it.*

Stuart: I can't place it. Italian, I suppose.

Shrubsole: The Chevalier is served.

He fills the glasses. **Stuart** *eats ravenously as* **Shrubsole** *serves* **Dr. Sobieska**.

Dr. Sobieska: *(quietly, so that the others cannot hear)* I think we've landed him, darling.

Shrubsole: His wife is dead against us.

Dr. Sobieska: I know, but I think he'll come to New York.

Shrubsole: You really think so?

Dr. Sobieska: Positive.

Shrubsole: Poppet – I hate to say this –

Dr. Sobieska: Be scientific, Bibi – be objective.

Shrubsole: Well – you haven't held out any inducements, have you?

Dr. Sobieska: Bibi, you thrust a sword into my heart!

Shrubsole: I simply had to ask.

Dr. Sobieska: I swear to you, Bibi, on my sacred honour as a scientist, everything that passed in there was simply – field work.

Stuart: Give me more of that omelet!

Shrubsole: At once, Chevalier.

He deftly puts **Dr. Sobieska**'*s untouched portion in front of* **Stuart**, *to her dismay. She never gets any of it.*

Stuart: Is this not the finest omelet you ever tasted, cousin? I do not ask for flattery, but merely for a corroboration of my own infallible judgement. Is this not perfection?

Dr. Sobieska: I cannot contradict you, Sire. *(to* **Shrubsole***)* Bibi, I am hungry.

Shrubsole: After what you have gone through for science, poppet, you surely don't grudge an omelet?

Dr. Sobieska: After what I have gone through for science, I want steak!

Shrubsole: Perhaps they have some. I'll take a look.

Lilian: I will not allow you to ransack this house for comforts for that adulteress.

Shrubsole: Madam, that's a hard word.

Lilian: Ben, I appeal to you. Stop this charade and turn these people out!

Stuart: Keep off, Walkinshaw. I won't be plagued while I'm eating.

Lilian: Don't call me that! Ben – Ben, I beg you, stop this pretense. I'll forgive everything; I'll never mention tonight as long as we live, but you just get these people out of this house!

Stuart: Walkinshaw, I can hardly understand a word you say. You sound like someone hallooing down a chimney. If you can't speak plainly, woman, have the goodness to hold your tongue.

Lilian: *(seizing him by the arm and shaking it)* Ben, I've been loyal to you through thick and thin, but this is more than I can tolerate! I'll leave you! I swear I will! I'll –

Calmly, but powerfully, he throws her from him, and as she staggers toward the wall he throws a dirty plate at her head, which fortunately shatters on the wall behind her. He speaks coldly.

Stuart: You bepoxed old strumpet, how dare you lay your hand on the Lord's anointed. Leave me! You'll leave me, you saucy trull, when I give you leave to go, and not before. Now be silent.

He turns to his bottle of wine, which he proceeds methodically to drink; **Shrubsole** *and* **Dr. Sobieska** *go to* **Lilian**'s *assistance.* **Clemmie** *brings her a glass of water.*

Clemmie: Here, Lil, take a sip o' this. Would you like me to make you some tea?

Lilian: No. I'll find another way. I'll bring him to himself –

Shrubsole: I told you it was dangerous to try that. Can't you understand that he is not the man you know as your husband?

Lilian: That's a lie. This whole thing is a trick, a plot to humiliate me! But I won't be tricked! I'm better stuff than you think, whatever-your-name-is. I don't know why you are doing this, but I won't give in to it. I'm going to fight!

Dr. Sobieska: Please, I beg of you, give up any idea of fighting; it can only make the greatest trouble for us all. I understand this situation as you cannot. If fighting had been the solution, do you think I would have let myself be carried away as I was?

Lilian: Yes, I do! You enjoyed it! You're the kind of woman who would. That's probably what you came for.

Dr. Sobieska: Madam, you go too far!

Lilian: You came here to steal my husband. Why, I cannot imagine, but that was obviously your intention.

Dr. Sobieska: Your husband? Permit me to state some facts, madam –

Shrubsole: Now, now, poppet; we must be as scientific and objective as possible.

Dr. Sobieska: That is precisely what I intend to do. That piece of flesh whom you claim as your husband is at this moment the Chevalier St. George, Bonnie Prince Charlie, the Young Pretender; he is also, when my husband and I have him under laboratory conditions, James the Third, Charles the First, and Jamie the Saxt o' Scotland.

Lilian: Rubbish! When he is not under your vile drug he is my husband.

Dr. Sobieska: No! He is of royal blood, and he was baptised a Catholic. Your marriage is therefore no marriage at all, and the highest compliment we can pay your association is to call it morganatic.

Lilian: Morganatic!

Dr. Sobieska: You are his mistress, madam, and a mistress with the hectoring, possessive, self-assertive airs of a North American *bourgeoise*.

Lilian: You will not bamboozle me with insults. Whatever your purpose is, you will never persuade me that my husband is not my husband, at this moment, as he has been for nearly twenty years.

Fred: Does he look exactly like your husband, Mrs. Stuart?

Carol: Fred, don't be stupid.

Fred: Carol, don't interfere. I suppose you haven't noticed that since he changed he's been left-handed? Look at him now.

Lilian: And I suppose you'll tell me that all the Stuarts were left-handed.

Shrubsole: No, but Charles Edward was. I'm afraid that you must admit his undoubted royalty.

Lilian: No. I must have something more substantial than the conduct of a ruffian to convince me of that.

Shrubsole: As you wish. Perhaps it can be managed.

Dr. Sobieska: Bibi, what are you thinking of?

Shrubsole: The Royal Touch. He spoke of it himself. *(to* **Lilian***)* You have heard of it? For centuries the kings of England touched the sick and cured many of them. After the deposition of the Stuarts the custom fell into disuse, for the very good reason that the Hanoverians seemed not to have the knack of it. The Touch was usually given for scrofula, which isn't a very common disease now, but it was efficacious for many things. If he were to touch someone, and that person were to be benefited, even momentarily, would you take that as a sign of royalty?

Lilian: You call yourself a scientist! Do you believe that?

Shrubsole: I call myself a scientist, but that does not mean that I disbelieve everything I have not seen. I am offering to take a very great risk in order to prove my point.

Lilian: And whom would he Touch?

Shrubsole: Yourself, perhaps? Have you any affection of the skin, any persistent ailment –

Lilian: Certainly not. I am here to be convinced, not to lend myself to such mummery.

Clemmie: Let me! Let me! I've got this rheumatism –

Lilian: No! you are a professional testifier to cures. Anybody and anything could cure you.

Clemmie: Yes, but I've had this bad hand for years, and –

Lilian: Certainly not!

Clemmie: Well, I call it pretty small!

Shrubsole: Who else? Mr. Lewis? Miss Stuart?

Clemmie: Carol'd be a good one.

Carol: There's nothing wrong with me.

Fred: Well, you're always complaining about something.

Clemmie: Think, Carol; everybody's got something wrong, if they'll just **think**.

Fred: We've got to find somebody.

Carol: Why? I don't see that it means anything to you.

Fred: Yes it does. I want to see the experiment. If you're so healthy we'll have to bring in somebody from outside.

Lilian: We shall certainly do nothing of the kind.

Fred: Carol, I don't think you want this experiment to be tried. Are you afraid that it will succeed?

Carol: I don't want to get an old house over my head. Can't you understand that?

Fred: It seems pretty clear that we've all got old houses over our heads whether we like it or not. You're scared of being royal, is that it? You're afraid of the truth. That's the most dangerous kind of stupidity.

Carol: Oh, don't be so pompous!

Fred: I don't intend to live all my life on my knees, and if you want to stay smaller than your natural size you do it alone, so far as I'm concerned.

Dr. Sobieska: The Chevalier is becoming drowsy!

Shrubsole: There isn't much time before the dose will wear off. We must be quick. It'll have to be Mrs. Izzard, whatever the objections. What's your trouble?

Clemmie: Well, it's my hands. You see, the left hand hasn't really been able to straighten out for three or four years.

Shrubsole: Looks like arthritis. Sure you can't straighten it? That's a searching test for the Royal Touch or anything else. But we must hurry. Go to him, poppet.

Dr. Sobieska: I hope you were pleased with your omelet, Sire?

Stuart: Well enough pleased, cousin. But I have been puzzled by this wine. *(He holds up the empty bottle.)* It reminds me of Scotland yet how can that be? There is no wine in Scotland. But there is a berry that grows there, that I have eaten on the moors, that tastes like this. Tastes and smells, cousin, are the keys of memory.

She engages him in conversation, obviously to keep him awake, and, as they continue to talk, **Shrubsole** *directs the others.*

Shrubsole: Have you any candles?

Lilian: We have ornamental candles. They are not intended to be lit.

Shrubsole: *(to* **Carol***)* Get them. Get all you can – even short ends. Put 'em in saucers or bottles if you haven't enough sticks. And a cushion. This'll have to do. We'll put it here. Fred, we must have a royal chaplain. Any clergymen among your ancestors?

Fred: A few. Plymouth Brethren, mostly.

Shrubsole: Never mind. Get a sheet from the bedroom, and be quick – hurry with the candles – Mrs. Stuart, may I borrow your Bible?

Lilian: I am not sure that I want to further this experiment, as you call it –

Shrubsole: Oh, very well; if you haven't got a Bible –

She goes into the bedroom as **Fred** *emerges from it with a clean, folded sheet.* **Carol** *has found seven candles – 'ornamentals,' candle ends and a paraffin dip – and has mustered them in holders and bottles on the kitchen counter.*

Seven. Couldn't be better.

He arranges them, three on either side of the area where he has placed the cushion. Then he drapes **Fred**'s *sheet about him like a clerical surplice and, with sudden inspiration, whisks a 'runner' off a table and drapes it round* **Fred**'s *neck, like a stole. He gives him the seventh candle.*

There. You'll do. Carol, get some warm water in a basin and a clean hand towel. Use the best china basin you've got.

Lilian *has returned with her Bible;* **Shrubsole** *blows quite a lot of dust off it, and finds a place.*

Now, Fred, when I give the word, read this. And don't stop till I tell you. Are you ready with the basin and towel?

Carol: Yes.

Shrubsole: Well, madam, we are ready. Before we proceed, I want you to know that I have no more notion of what may come of this than you have yourself. I beg you to believe that. And whatever may happen I ask you not to interfere. If it's any satisfaction to you to know it, you have made me leap to a point I had not expected to reach for a year or more, and then under very different conditions. *(He goes about the room and turns out the two or three lamps that are in it, leaving only a central light. Then, going to* **Stuart**, *he kneels.)* Sire, may I intercede for your grace on behalf of a woman, a loyal subject of yours, who begs for the Royal Touch?

Stuart: Eh? I haven't Touched for many years. You're a physician, are you not? My cousin's physician? Do you believe in the Touch?

Shrubsole: Would I ask for it, Sire, if I did not?

Stuart: Not many people want a Pretender's Touch.

Dr. Sobieska: Who should know better than yourself, Sire, that kingship is not a matter of the crown, but of the spirit?

Stuart: That's very well said, cousin. Kingship is of the spirit. I'll do it.

Shrubsole: *(softly)* Now, Fred.

Fred: *(Reads, as* **Shrubsole** *turns out the last electric light in the room. In the candlelight, the cheapness and trumpery ornament disappears, and only the bones of the setting are visible; thus revealed, the old house has its own nobility.)* The king shall joy in thy strength, O Lord; and in thy salvation how greatly shall he rejoice! Thou hast given him his heart's desire, and hast not withholden the request of his lips. Selah.

Dr. Sobieska *has guided* **Stuart** *to his place by the cushion upon which, at* **Shrubsole**'*s bidding,* **Clemmie** *is about to kneel.* **Fred**'*s reading continues beneath the dialogue.*

Stuart: But this is my nurse, my earliest friend, and the guardian of my childhood: why did no one tell me that you were ailing, my dear?

He signs to **Clemmie** *to kneel;* **Shrubsole** *takes the bowl and towel, and offers them to* **Stuart**, *kneeling;* **Stuart** *washes and dries his hands; then, as* **Clemmie** *holds her gnarled left hand up to him, he touches it lightly with his own left hand and, moved, leans forward and kisses her cheek. Meanwhile the voice of* **Fred** *continues.*

Fred: For thou preventest him with the blessings of goodness: thou settest a crown of pure gold on his head. He asked life of thee and thou gavest it him, even length of days for ever and ever. His glory is great in thy salvation: honour and majesty hast thou laid upon him. For thou hast made him most blessed forever: thou hast made him exceedingly glad with thy countenance. For the king trusteth in the Lord, and through the mercy of the Most High he shall not be moved. Thine hand shall find out all thine enemies: thy right hand shall find out those that hate thee.

As **Fred** *reads,* **Clemmie** *remains on her knees, her head bent; then slowly, she raises it, and we see that her face is wet with tears; she holds up the twisted hand toward* **Stuart**, *and it is now straight; she moves the fingers in wonderment.*

Clemmie: Oh Ben! Ben!

Stuart *sways, then falls to the ground;* **Clemmie**, *who is already kneeling,* *takes his head in her lap, and* **Shrubsole** *bathes his face with the towel and water which he has been holding.* **Fred**, *who has continued reading from the Twenty-first Psalm, breaks off here.*

Shrubsole: He'll be around in a minute. And he'll be the man you've known. He's perfectly all right.

Like **Fred** *in Act Two,* **Stuart** *sighs, and opens his eyes.*

Stuart: Have I been asleep? Aren't you the people from New York? The Coffin Foundation? Yes, I remember now. Well – how did I behave?

Shrubsole: You'll remember most of it in a little while.

Stuart: But was I satisfactory? Was I a good Guinea Pig?

Shrubsole: More satisfactory than we dared to hope.

Stuart: Well then, Lil, which is it to be – London or New York?

Lilian *has been moving about the room, turning on the electric light and quenching the candles.*

Lilian: Neither, I think.

Stuart: Oh? Was I as bad as that? Was I an oddity, like Fred?

Dr. Sobieska: You mustn't make any decision for a few days. At any time now you will begin to remember your experiences of the past two hours. *(He gazes at her in recognition.)* At the Coffin Foundation, of course, things would not be quite like that. Here we had to work with the materials that lay to hand, so to speak. But I can assure you that life would be very pleasant with us – very pleasant. And you would be making a distinguished contribution to science, Chevalier.

Stuart: Chevalier! Yes, of course; I begin to remember. *(He looks from* **Lilian** *to* **Dr. Sobieska**, *and back to* **Lilian** *again.)*

Shrubsole: In honesty I must point out, sir, that it wouldn't be all beer and skittles. But I can promise you that it would be very interesting. We won't press for an answer, but we shall be at the Chateau Laurier for a few days, and you can always reach us by telephone. And now, sir, I think we had better leave you to a night's rest.

Stuart: Oh, don't go! I'd like to talk the whole affair over at length.

Shrubsole: It will be better if we are not here when full recollection comes to you. You see, among other pleasures, you had two bottles of Scotch and a bottle of loganberry wine in quite a short time. You may feel that, in half an hour.

Fred: I'll take you to your hotel, if you like. You, too, Mrs. Izzard.

Dr. Sobieska: That would be very kind. Are we to understand that you have lost your prejudice against the study of heredity?

Fred: What would you expect? I'm not a bigot, I hope. Heredity is the old house we all have over our heads; environment is the junk we put in it. See you tomorrow, Carol.

Carol: Maybe.

Fred: I said I'd see you tomorrow.

Shrubsole: *(with formal geniality, as though nothing unusual had happened)* Goodbye, Mrs. Stuart. Very sorry to have kept you from your club.

Dr. Sobieska: Chevalier, whatever your decision may be, I should like you to keep the Young Pretender's snuffbox. It is rightfully yours.

Stuart: You are very kind. Goodnight, Clemmie dear. *(He kisses her, and she strokes his face adoringly.)* Take good care of the Flush-of-Youth Lady.

Shepherded by **Fred,** *they go.* **Lilian** *immediately goes into the bedroom.* **Carol** *comes to* **Stuart.**

Carol: Father, you won't go, will you?

Stuart: Why are you so anxious?

Carol: We're not royal. I mean, it's so silly. It was a trick of some sort. I don't want to be royal. Not that I would be, of course, but if the idea got around, people would expect all kinds of things from me – **you** know. I want to be just ordinary.

Stuart: Well, Kitty, in spite of environment and heredity and all that, I suppose what one is always remains very much a matter of choice. If you really want to be ordinary, I don't suppose anything can stop you.

Carol: That business with Clemmie – it doesn't exactly make you a king, does it? I mean, she loves you so much that you could do anything with her.

Stuart: Perhaps that, multiplied by thousands, is what it means to be a king.

Carol: Maybe, but the time for all that has gone.

Stuart: So everybody says.

Carol: *(kissing him)* I knew you'd see it the sensible way. Anyhow, you're number one C.I.P., and that's quite a distinction, isn't it? If you went to New York to those people, you'd be a kind of prisoner, wouldn't you? It means a lot to be free, doesn't it? Goodnight, Daddy. *(She goes.)*

Stuart: Lil, what are you doing?

Lilian: *(from the bedroom)* I'm tidying this room. I'd be glad of your help.

Stuart: In a minute. I'll tidy a bit in here, first.

He moves about the room, turning out the lights until only that which comes faintly in from the bedroom is left, and clear November moonlight floods in through the windows. Once again the handsome structure of the old house is seen, and the hideous furnishing is bathed in kindly oblivion. **Stuart** *stands by the window, and we see that he has in his hand the handsome genealogical chart which* **Shrubsole** *has left behind: he looks at it, then lays it aside and takes from the pocket of his gown the Young Pretender's snuffbox. He runs his fingers caressingly over it, and we hear him speak to himself.*

A kind of prisoner ... well, we'll see about that.

He moves downstage in the moonlight, finds a number in the telephone directory, and dials it.

British Airways? I want a passage on your next flight to Scotland ... Tonight, if possible.... Yes, it is urgent – Government business – oh yes, on the highest level.

He smiles as the Curtain falls.

The Voice
of the People

The Voice of the People

Characters:

Sam North

Aggie Morton

Shorty Morton

Myrtle Morton

(The scene is the kitchen of **Shorty Morton***'s house. Though it has no special charm it is plainly the most lived-in room in the house, and as well as the usual kitchen equipment there are a few home-like touches such as a plant growing in a tin can which has been partly disguised with water-stained crepe paper. One entrance is from the "front room" and the other from the back porch.*

When the curtain rises **Sam North***, an electrician, lies on his back, working at the entrails of the electric stove. He is a good workman and a man of considerable character.* **Aggie Morton** *watches him in a condition of dreary anxiety.)*

Aggie: What Shorty will say when he finds he can't have a hot meal I just don't like to think.

Sam: Nothing he says can hurry this job.

Aggie: Well, he always wants his meals prompt, you know.

Sam: So do I, but I won't get my supper till this job is done, and I'm not complaining.

Aggie: You're not Shorty. "What'd the Lord give me a tongue for if not to make my wants known?" he says.

Sam: The Lord gave us all tongues, but we don't all use 'em the same way.

Aggie: That's just what I say to him. "The Lord gave you a tongue to sing His praises," I say, "and I wish you'd do it." You ever visit the tabernacle?

Sam: Wired it.

Aggie: What?

Sam: I said I wired it. I put in all those spotlights that shine on the pulpit.

Aggie: Did you? Now isn't that interesting. They're awful pretty. And do you know, when Pastor Beamis gets up to the pinnacle of his exhortation, they seem to shine brighter than ever.

Sam: Rheostat.

Aggie: Hm?

Sam: Rheostat in the pulpit. He works it by hand, out of sight. Increases the power.

Aggie: Well now, I don't think it's nice of you to tell a thing like that.

Sam: Nice or not, it's a fact. I do what I'm told and I do an honest job. What happens after that's no affair of mine.

Aggie: Well, there are some things which should be kept from unbelievers and scoffers, like Shorty. Shorty doesn't like Pastor Beamis. Says he doesn't get his hair cut often enough.

Sam: If he didn't have lots of white hair he wouldn't have anything for those spotlights to shine on. Nobody wants to see fifteen hundred watts glaring down on a bald head.

Aggie: I know, but Shorty has a professional interest in hair, and he doesn't see things the way just anybody would. Oh, I can hear him now; I always know the way his wheel bumps on the curb.

There is whistling outside and a voice cries, "I'm home, Ag," and **Shorty** *bustles in. He has a somewhat over-elaborate arrangement of hair, and the perfection of his shave is the envy of lesser men. He need not be uncommonly short, but his bustling ways and cocksure manner suggest shortness – not entirely a physical shortness.*

Shorty: Well, what's for supper?

Aggie: Hello, hon; aren't you early?

Shorty: Nope. What's for supper?

Aggie: Well, to tell you the truth, hon, nothing's for supper yet.

Shorty: Eh? Why? I could eat a horse.

Aggie: Well, it's the stove again.

Shorty: I could eat a horse and chase the rider. What's wrong with the stove?

Aggie: It broke down again, and I had to get Mr. North to come, and he didn't get here till late, and it won't be done for quite a while, hon, so you see I couldn't get you any supper.

Shorty: No supper! A fine thing! I work like a beaver all day – standing up, fidgety, pernickety work – till I'm all used up, and when I come home, then what? No supper!

Aggie: Sure, I know hon. I know just how you feel. But it don't happen often.

Shorty: Seems to me it happened just the other day.

Aggie: Oh hon, that was three months ago, and it was the stove that time, too. We got to face it, hon; sooner or later we'll just have to get a new stove.

Shorty: Sure! Get after me for a new stove! I come home, done right out after a hard day, no supper's ready, and I'm weakened. So now's the time to hound me for a new stove!

Aggie: Aw hon, you know I don't mean it like that. But the stove's done, honest it is. Ask Mr. North.

Shorty: Yeah, he's a fine one to ask. His firm sells stoves. If you want a fair, unprejudiced opinion on your old stove, ask a man who's got stoves to sell. Yeah!

Sam: Now then, Shorty, you don't have to talk to me like that. I'm not married to you, you know.

Shorty: And what do you mean by that?

Sam: I mean that you may be a martyr to your wife, but to me you're just a barber with an empty belly. If you want me to finish this stove tonight, don't give me any of your lip. It's nothing to me whether you eat or not.

Shorty: Well all right, all right. Can't a man open his mouth in his own house?

Sam: Just don't open it too wide, that's all. I can fix this stove, and I can go on fixing it, but Mrs. Morton's right; you'd be better off to get a new one.

Shorty *opens his mouth to reply, thinks better of it, and shuts his mouth again.*

Aggie: Would you like something cold, hon? A baloney sandwich?

Shorty: *(a martyr)* No. I'll wait. The repair man is doing his best, I suppose. Anyway, you know my stomach. Can't touch baloney any way but fried. Paper come yet?

Aggie: Not yet, hon.

Shorty: Everything's late tonight – if I can say so in my own house without giving offence.

Aggie: Seems to me that boy gets later and later every night.

Shorty: Well, what'd I tell you? When he wants his money on Friday, dock him a cent for every night he's late.

Aggie: I told him that, and he said he'd stop bringing the paper if I did.

Shorty: Well of all the nerve! Don't know what gets into kids these days. All right, let him stop the paper. Never anything in it, anyhow.

Aggie: Inspector Higgins said at the last Home and School Club meeting that the daily paper is a daily page of history.

Shorty: Oh he did, eh? And I suppose that picture of his daughter's wedding that was in last month hadn't anything at all to do with it? Oh no! I guess not! There's wheels within wheels. Anyway, who's Higgins? He's a civic employee, ain't he? Who's he, to be going around shooting off his face? When I want any advice from him, I'll ask for it.

Aggie: Well, hon, they did ask him to address the Home and School.

Shorty: All right, then; he ought to keep off controversial topics. A public servant has no right to an opinion on any subject that's got two sides to it.

(A thump is heard outside on the porch.)

Aggie: There's the paper. I'll get it.

Shorty: No, I'll get it. I want to speak to that boy. *(He goes, and is heard outside.)* It's about time you got here: why don't you trade that wheel for a tortoise? You'd be faster!

Paper Boy's Voice: Aw, go peel a prune, will ya?

Shorty: *(re-entering)* D'you hear that? Can't get a civil word out of these modern kids. Not that he's any kid. "Junior merchants" they call 'em now! Why that kid needed a shave!

Aggie: Aw now, hon; you're just funning.

Shorty: No, I mean it. All kids ought to shave earlier. I was shaving every day when I was fourteen. It's hygienic. They ought to teach it in the schools.

Aggie: Aw go on!

Shorty: No funnier than a lot of the stuff they do teach.

Sam: How about teaching them to cut their own hair?

Shorty: *(sourly)* Ha! ha! very funny.

Aggie: Can I see the paper?

Shorty: Let me take a look through it, first. It don't take me long to find out what's in it. Local page first.

His daughter **Myrtle** *enters; she is a morose girl of sixteen, indifferent to her family. It is noticeable that* **Aggie**'*s tone to* **Myrtle** *is hectoring, in contrast to her deferential air toward* **Shorty**. *This is called Being a Careful Mother.*

Myrtle: Sorry to be late for supper again, Mom.

Aggie: Well, as it so happens, you're not late. No supper for anybody till the stove's fixed.

Myrtle *puts her schoolbooks on the refrigerator or a side table, sits down, and unfolds a movie magazine.*

Aggie: You don't seem to mind much.

Myrtle: I can wait.

Aggie: Been stuffing yourself at the ice cream parlour, I suppose.

Myrtle: Mom, nobody's called them parlours for about two hundred years. They're bars, now. Soda bars.

Aggie: Fine name, I must say. Pastor Beamis says names are very important. A bad name is halfway to making a bad thing, he says.

Myrtle: Pastor Beamis gives me a pain where it don't show.

Aggie: Myrtle Morton! You've been out with boys again!

Myrtle: So what!

Aggie: I can always tell. You come home full of bold talk and bold talk'll make a bold girl of you, and do you know what happens to bold girls?

Shorty: *(from behind the paper)* The Simpson girl's had her baby, I see.

Aggie: Eh? Well, and about time, it seems to me. Boy or girl?

Shorty: Girl.

Aggie: Oh well, maybe the next one'll be a boy. (**Myrtle** *does not appreciate this remark.*) Now listen, Myrtle, how often do I have to tell you that a girl's first job is to keep herself sweet? A sweet girl will outstrip a bold girl, in the end. You mind what I tell you.

Myrtle: Uh-huh.

Aggie: I've been a girl, and I know a girl's problems. Boldness seems like fun, but sweetness pays off in the end, in the form of a lovely home and a husband that respects you. Not for years, of course. Don't go getting any notions.

Shorty: Say, this is a terrible paper. Half these sport reports are so skimpy they don't mean a thing. It's a crime what they get away with.

Aggie: Myrtle, what about your homework?

Myrtle: Done.

Aggie: Oh. When?

Myrtle: I had a couple of study periods this afternoon. Did it then.

Aggie: Well I don't like to see you with one of those screen magazines when you got school work to do.

Myrtle: Oh Mom, remind me in the morning, will you? I got to take some objects to school.

Aggie: What objects?

Myrtle: Oh, clock springs, and corks, and silver paper, and a little piece of fur if you've got it. You know: junk.

Aggie: What in the world for?

Myrtle: Art.

Aggie: What kind of art?

Myrtle: Oh, we have to make an arrangement. We each get a box, and we have to bring some junk and arrange it interestingly in the box. It's to show if we have a sense of form, or something. The best box gets a prize. A book by a painter. Sounds like an Irishman, from his name. Salvador Daley.

Aggie: Well who ever heard the like of that?

Sam: Maybe Shorty's right. They ought to teach 'em to shave.

Shorty: You know, the funnies get worse every day. Wish they'd bring back Mutt and Jeff. I don't know why I read this paper at all. Not a thing in it.

Sam: Anything new on the conference?

Shorty: What conference?

Sam: The international trade conference.

Shorty: Aw, I never read that stuff. It's all in the hands of the big interests. Can't believe a word of it.

He has discarded the paper, through which **Aggie** *is now browsing with a great rustling of leaves, for she is a dishevelled reader.*

Myrtle: What's the weather forecast, Mom?

Aggie: Uh: fair and warm.

Shorty: Get out your umbrella, then. They always get the weather wrong.

Sam: You haven't much use for the paper, have you, Shorty?

Shorty: Nope. Don't trust 'em. Controlled by their advertisers.

Sam: Oh.

Shorty: Yeah. Common knowledge. Wheels within wheels.

Sam: I read it pretty carefully. Especially foreign news. Trouble comes so fast, nowadays, you want to spot it while it's a long way off.

Shorty: Yeah? Well, do you know what I'd do if I was in the driver's seat? I'd just tell these foreigners right where they get off, in plain words. Then we'd have no more bother with 'em. I never read that stuff. You can't depend on it.

Aggie: You know, the part of the paper I like best are these bits they print at the bottom of the columns to fill up. Now listen to this: "The piccolo is a small flute, pitched an octave higher than the large concert flute."

Shorty: So what?

Aggie: Well, it's something to remember. Here's another: "The world's greatest ocean, the Pacific, has an area of 67,699,630 square miles." Imagine.

Shorty: A fellow came in for a haircut, couple of weeks ago, said you could put the whole of Australia in Lake Ontario, and still have a good-sized lake.

Aggie: Was he from Australia?

Shorty: No, from out in the country, someplace.

Myrtle: Miss White says there's a Chinaman born every time the clock ticks.

Aggie: I don't believe it, not after what I went through with you! Sixteen hours, I was.

Myrtle: Well, she teaches geography.

Aggie: Here's a good one. You know, if a person read all these every night, they'd soon have a first-class education. Listen: "The word mess, as used in such phrases as 'officer's mess' originally meant a portion of food –"

Shorty: Say, my stomach thinks my throat's cut! Sam! Sam!

Sam: *(from beneath the stove)* Speak, Lord, for Thy servant heareth.

Shorty: Eh?

Sam: Bible. What do you want?

Shorty: How much longer do you expect to be before we can use that stove?

Sam: Maybe half an hour.

Shorty: Can I help you?

Sam: No. Keep away.

Shorty: Aw!

The telephone rings. **Myrtle** *leaps for it, but* **Shorty** *forestalls her.*

Shorty: No you don't. *(In 'phone.)* Yeah. Oh, hello, Bill. No. No. What's eating you? No, you can't depend on a thing it says. Oh well, I looked at it, y'know, but I didn't actually read it. What? There is? About prices? He does? You bet we've got to reply. We've got to lash right out. We've got to strike while the iron is hot. Me? Why me? Well, call Jerry. You have? Say, what is this? Oh. Oh. Oh. Well, all right, but you know me. If I do it, it'll be a sizzler. Yeah, it'll be a scorcher. You leave it to me. Yeah. G'bye. *(He hangs up the telephone and turns to* **Aggie**, *who has been listening to every word.)* Gimme that paper! I'll peel his hide right offa him!

Aggie: Why, whatever's happened, hon?

Shorty: He can't blacken a whole profession. Money isn't everything.

Aggie: But what's happened?

Shorty: That was Bill. And d'you know what? There's a letter in the paper tonight crabbing about the increase in barber-shop prices. And who wrote it? That old snake-in-the-grass Townsend, that's who! Oh boy, what I'm going to do to him!

Aggie: Now, hon, you're not going to get into any fight or anything, are you?

Shorty: The boys want me to write a reply, that's what.

Aggie: They do?

Shorty: Yeah. The pen is mightier than the sword. You ought to know that, Ag. That's in the Bible.

Sam: No.

Shorty: Eh?

Sam: Not in the Bible. I was brought up on the Bible. Read it through three times before I was eighteen. That's not in it.

Shorty: I didn't ask you whether it was or not. Now don't bother me any more, any of you, because I got work to do. Y'know, it's a shame there isn't a room in this house where I can be private when I have an important job like this.

Aggie: Why hon, you can use the front room.

Shorty: *(who doesn't really want to go elsewhere)* No table.

Aggie: I'll set up the card table.

Shorty: Light's bad in there.

Aggie: How about our bedroom?

Shorty: Doesn't smell right for literary work. Nope, I'll have to manage right here. Only I don't want to be disturbed, see? So everybody keep quiet, see?

Aggie: Yes, hon.

Shorty: What about paper?

Aggie: Well, I've got some of my Boudoir Bond left. I'll get it. *(She goes into the "front room.")*

Shorty: Give me your pen, Myrt.

Myrtle: Go easy, I just got that nib the way I want it.

Shorty: What do you think I'm going to do? Pry up boards with it?

Myrtle: You got an awful heavy hand with a pen.

Shorty: Say, if I had a heavy hand, would I be the close shaver I am?

Myrtle: I don't know. My pen's no razor. Go easy.

Shorty: Don't know what gets into kids today. Criticize, criticize, all the time.

Aggie *returns with a box of "gift" paper.*

Aggie: Here you are, hon.

Shorty: Let's see. Oh hell, Ag, I can't use this!

Aggie: Why?

Shorty: It's got wiggly edges and the envelopes are lined with wallpaper! This is women's stuff!

Aggie: Well of course, hon. What did you expect? But it's nice paper. Look what it says: "Styled for milady's boudoir to personalize milady's correspondence." It smells, too. Smell, hon. Violets.

Shorty: Fooh! Take it away! How can I write a business letter on that?

Sam: Oh they'd just think you spilled some hair tonic on it.

Shorty: Reading the Bible three times didn't teach you to keep your nose out of other people's business, did it?

Sam: No.

Shorty: *(with dignity)* Well just oblige me by not interrupting, will you?

Sam: Okay, Shorty.

Shorty: Morton's the name. Mr. Morton.

Sam: *(unimpressed)* Uh-huh.

Shorty: What other paper have we got?

Aggie: Well I don't think there is any, except Myrtle's school paper.

Shorty: What you got, Myrt?

Myrtle: Nothing that'd be any good.

Shorty: Say look: I got to have paper, see? Now gimme some paper and be quick about it. *(Sees **Myrtle**'s schoolbooks on the refrigerator.)* I'll look myself. Say, here's a candy bar. Just what I need.

Myrtle: Aw, Dad, I got that to eat tonight listening to the Hour of Romance.

Shorty: Sugar. Quick energy. Just what I need. *(Eats.)* Here, this'll do. It's ruled kind of funny, but it'll do.

Myrtle: That's my graph paper!

Shorty: You can get some more. Now let's see. Begin with the date. Yeah. Then what? To the editor?

Sam: Send it to The Voice of the People.

Shorty: Is that right?

Sam: That's the department. The Voice of the People. Comes from a quotation, "The voice of the people is the voice of God."

Shorty: Oh yeah. The Bible.

Sam: Nope.

Aggie: Oh no, hon. God wrote the Bible Himself. You wouldn't catch Him putting anything like that in it.

Shorty: Well I don't care what you say, it's in the Bible, and if it ain't it ought to be because it's the truth. "The voice of the people is the voice of God." The voice of the people – that's me.

Sam: Modest, ain't you?

Shorty: Who is the people, if not me?

Sam: Well, me, for one.

Shorty: You're not writing this letter. Now let's have it quiet. Say, how do you begin?

Sam: Dear Sir.

Shorty: Oh I don't know. Sounds too friendly. How about "See here!"

Sam: Have it your own way.

Shorty: Myrt, you ought to know all this stuff.

Myrtle: They just teach us the Friendly Letter, the Congratulation or Condolence, and Applying for a Position.

Shorty: The trouble with modern education is it ain't practical. It don't fit kids for the problems of life. But I didn't get where I am by asking every Tom, Dick and Harry for advice. I'll write it my way.

He sets himself to the task of writing, which he pursues during the subsequent passages of dialogue with many bodily contortions, scratchings of himself, and occasional furious application of his pocket comb.

Aggie: What'd you pay for that magazine, Myrt?

Myrtle: Fifteen cents.

Shorty: Sh-h-h-h-h-h!

Aggie *pantomimes despair at such reckless expense.*

Sam: Will you try that right-hand front element, please?

Aggie *does so, and there is a certain amount of clicking of switches, and whispering between her and* **Sam**, *who drops a heavy pair of pliers with a thump.* **Shorty** *pantomimes literary anguish.* **Aggie** *approaches him with disturbing caution, and tries to read what he has written over his shoulder. At last –*

Shorty: Ag, quit breathing on me. Sit down.

Aggie: Well, will you promise to read us your letter when it's finished?

Shorty: Yeah. Now sit down.

A pause, broken only by **Shorty**'s *rough handling of Myrtle's fountain pen, which he bangs on the table to make the ink flow; he mops up the resulting mess with a tea towel.*

Myrtle: Mom, why can't I have a two-piece bathing suit?

Aggie: Because it calls attention to your bust, that's why.

Myrtle: Other girls have busts.

Aggie: Well, you're not going to have one, and that's that!

Myrtle: *(softly)* Aw, cheese and rice!

Aggie: Myrtle Morton! Did I hear you blaspheme?

Myrtle: *(innocently)* I only said "cheese and rice," Mom. It's just an expression. I might just as easy have said "rice and cheese."

Aggie: That's what comes of chumming with boys! You just pick up a lot o' bad. Why can't you chum with a nice girl?

Myrtle: 'Cause all the nice girls are chumming with boys.

Aggie: Oh, you just want to be provoking!

Shorty: Say, can't a man have a little quiet in his own house?

Aggie: Quiet now, Myrt, and don't bother your Dad!

Myrtle: Aw, cheese and rice!

Aggie *glares at her, but decides to pursue the point later. She picks up the paper and looks through it, rattling the pages and turning them inside out with the relish of a naturally noisy reader.*

Shorty: Ag.

Aggie: Yes, hon?

Shorty: Quit making that row with the paper, will you?

Aggie: What row?

Shorty: Aw, what's the use?

A pause, during which **Aggie** *re-folds the paper with irritating caution. Suddenly –*

Aggie: Oh hon!

Shorty: *(with cold rage)* What?

Aggie: The assessor called today. I just remembered.

Shorty: Did you let him in?

Aggie: No, I kept him on the porch all the time, like you said.

Shorty: Good.

Aggie: I just wanted to tell you while I remembered. If he'd seen that re-papering in the front room, I dread to think what he might have done.

Shorty: Ag.

Aggie: Eh?

Shorty: Sh-h-h-h!

A final agony, during which **Shorty** *is obviously in search of the right – the only possible – word. After two or three disappointments it comes to him with the force of a thunderbolt, and he finishes his letter in a burst of enthusiastic speed.*

Shorty: Well, that's that!

Aggie: Oh hon, let's hear it.

Shorty: Well, if you really want to.

Aggie: Of course we want to. Listen Myrt.

Shorty: Well – here goes. *(He reads, with vehemence.)* "Dear Sir: Say, that's a fine thing, calling it the Voice of the People when you print dirty attacks on the people by T.J. Townsend who hates the people's guts. The real people are behind the barbers, etcetera, a hundred per cent. A fair day's pay for a fair day's work. That's fair. May I ask what this snake-in-the-grass Townsend knows about the strain on a barber's feet, etcetera? Let's hear what our veterans, etcetera, have to say. And Townsend better not forget that the barbers know what he did with the corpse of his Uncle Matt. Thanking you for space, etcetera, Fair Play."

Aggie: Oh, hon, that's wonderful! That'll take the gimp out of Townsend, all right.

Shorty: If it's printed. Maybe it'll just be thrown in the wastebasket.

Aggie: Oh they wouldn't dare.

Shorty: Townsend's a pretty powerful man. The paper wouldn't want to offend him. There's wheels within wheels, you know. But d'you know what? If this isn't in the Voice of the People tomorrow night, I'll go right in and ask the editor why.

Aggie: That's right, hon. You stand up to them.

Myrtle: *(who has been looking over* **Shorty**'s *shoulder)* It's not very plain.

Shorty: Well, it's their business to make it out.

Myrtle: You haven't put your name on.

Shorty: "Fair Play" is enough. That's what you call a pseudonym. *(He pronounces it "swaydo-nime.")* That's Latin. From "Swaydo," meaning classy, like in suede shoes, and "nime" meaning name. There's a "p" in it, but only ignorant people pay any attention to it.

Aggie: I see. Like "nom de plume."

Shorty: That's French, of course, meaning "feather name"; a lot of Frenchmen still write with feathers. Cheap, I suppose. They got a very low standard of living.

Myrtle: Well it says in the paper you have to sign your name. Look. "No letters will be printed unless accompanied by the name and address of the sender, which will not be published if so desired."

Shorty: That's all right. I know all about that. The paper gets hold of your name, and where are you? No. "Fair Play's" enough.

Sam: Wouldn't it carry more weight if you signed your own name? A rip-snorter like that, I mean?

Shorty: Listen, I know what I'm doing. I don't want to show my hand too much in this thing just yet. I can't tell all I know, but you can take it from me that I have my reasons.

Aggie: Kind of power behind the throne.

Shorty: That's it, Ag.

Sam: Didn't Townsend sign his letter?

Shorty: Eh? Uh – let me see that paper, Myrt.

Myrtle: I can look. Only one letter in tonight, and it's signed "Pro Bono Publico."

Shorty: There! See? He didn't sign it.

Sam: Then how do you know who wrote it?

Shorty: Eh? Why because Bill told me, that's why! Townsend wrote to the paper, raising Cain because of the advance in barbershop prices –

Sam: Have you read the letter?

Shorty: Uh, no. As a matter of cold fact, no. But Bill told me all about it on the 'phone.

Sam: Don't you think it would be a good idea to read it?

Shorty: Well, maybe. Myrt –

Myrtle: I'll read it. "Sir: May I ask a question which has been bothering a lot of people lately, and which has not been answered by our politicians or the newspapers. It is this: if the Government can put a floor under prices whenever it likes, why is it called unwarrantable interference with business to put a ceiling on prices? Prices have gone up in everything from national business to small local business, and surely it is time to call a halt. Yours, Pro Bono Publico."

Sam: I didn't hear anything about barbershops in that.

Shorty: Oh, you didn't? What's that crack about "small business," then?

Sam: Might be any of a dozen things.

Shorty: Not a bit of it. Townsend's got it in for the barbers, and that's just his crafty way of trying to put us off the scent.

Sam: What I still can't figure out is what makes you so sure it was Townsend wrote it.

Shorty: Well, you don't know the ins and outs of the thing. If you did you'd know it couldn't be anybody else.

Sam: I'd want to be pretty sure, myself, before I got into a thing like that. You've mentioned Townsend by name in your letter, and you've hinted something or other about a corpse.

Shorty: Yeah, that's rich. That's the cream of it. *(Reads)* "And Townsend better not forget that the barbers know what he did with the corpse of his Uncle Matt." Ha ha! That'll burn him up!

Sam: It certainly suggests a variety of things to people who aren't in the know. You don't think the paper might consider it a little bit on the libellous side, do you?

Shorty: It's true. What's the libel in telling the truth?

Sam: Plenty, sometimes. But you don't tell anything. You just hint.

Aggie: Yes, that's true, hon. I don't know what Townsend did with the corpse, for one. Come on, tell us. Myrt, you go out and see if you can find a girl to chum with.

Myrtle: I want to hear, too.

Aggie: No you don't! Now out you go!

Myrtle: Dad, can't I hear? Please, Dad? After all, I'll be in Commercial next year.

Shorty: Well it's pretty raw, but I guess you can stay. It all happened last Fall, when Townsend's old Uncle Matt died. It was a Sunday morning, and Devlin the undertaker 'phoned Jim to go up and give Uncle Matt his last shave, before they embalmed him. Up Jim goes, and there was Townsend. Well, you know Townsend. He loves fifty cents better than he loves his right eye. "What's this shave going to cost?" he says. "Well," says Jim, "it's specialized work, and it's Sunday, and the price'll be five dollars." "Five dollars!" says Townsend, nearly choking. "That's what I said," says Jim. You know how cool Jim is. "Good morning," says Townsend, "I won't need you." And with that he shows Jim the door. And then d'you know what? He gets his own razor – a safety – and he shaves his Uncle Matt himself, and the old man as dead as Job's turkey, and from that day to this Townsend's had his knife into the barbers!

Aggie: Hon, he *never!*

Shorty: Without a word of a lie. The hired girl told Jim's sister.

Myrtle: I never knew a corpse had to be shaved.

Shorty: Well, it does, and the first half dozen I did, I can tell you, I just about bit the end right off my heart!

Sam: And that's what makes you so sure Townsend wrote that letter.

Shorty: Sure. "Pro Bono Publico." He can't fool me. What's it mean, any-way?

Sam: Latin.

Shorty: Myrt, you take Latin. What's it mean?

Myrtle: Don't know. It's not in our book.

Shorty: You can make a stab at it, can't you?

Myrtle: Well, "pro" means for – or maybe against. One or the other.

Shorty: Yeah, and "publico" means public.

Myrtle: No no. You mustn't try to translate Latin words by the English words they look like. Miss McGregor says you get all mixed up that way. If "publico" looks like public you can bet that's one thing it don't mean!

Shorty: Say, what they need at that school is a good course in common sense.

Sam: Well, I'd want to be surer than you are before I sent a letter like that to the paper.

Shorty: Listen, you're doing an awful lot of worrying about something that's none of your business. But just to show you, I'll call up the paper and ask 'em who wrote it.

Sam: That might be a good idea.

Shorty: *(at the telephone)* I wouldn't want you to lose any sleep worrying about it. Let's see. *(He operates the dial.)* Say listen, I want to ask a question. – Yes, I've got my paper. That's not what I phoned about. Say listen, I want the name of the fellow that wrote that letter that's in tonight signed "Pro Bono Publico." – Never you mind who's speaking. Just you tell me. – Oh, you don't, eh? Well you don't fool me for a minute. *(He slams down the telephone angrily, and speaks, imitating a woman's voice.)* "Sorry, only the editor has that information, and he has gone home." Stooges! Stooges for the big interests! But I know. They're covering up for Townsend!

Sam: Well, you can cook your supper now, I guess.

Aggie: Is it done?

Sam: Ought to last for a while, but all the wiring underneath is awful old.

Shorty: *(who has been addressing one of Aggie's despised envelopes)* Got a stamp, Ag?

Aggie: No. Used them all when I wrote to Mother.

Shorty: Myrt, got a stamp?

Myrtle: Only a couple of ones.

Shorty: Gimme them. It's a cent short, but if they have to pay two cents to get my letter at the paper it'll teach 'em to be civil to people on the 'phone.

Sam: Well, I'll get out of your way, now. Good night.

Shorty: Say, just drop this in the box as you pass the corner, will you?

Sam: Okay. Or I'll take it direct, if you'd rather.

Shorty: To the paper, you mean?

Sam: No, home. I guess it's for me, really. You see – I hate to disappoint you, Shorty – I'm "Pro Bono Publico." And here's one for you to chew on that *is* in the Bible: "He that answereth a matter before he heareth it, it is folly and shame unto him." Good night, all.

He goes, and **Shorty** *stares after him in stupefaction.*

Curtain

Biography
Robertson Davies, Playwright

In his distinguished literary career, Robertson Davies has collected almost
every honour possible: over twenty honorary degrees; a Governor
General's Award; the Lorne Pierce Medal for literary achievement; the
Stephen Leacock Award for Humour; the Medal of Honour for Literature
from the National Arts Club, New York; Booker and Nobel Prize nomina-
tions. He is a Member of the American Academy and Institute of Arts and
Letters, Fellow of the Royal Society of Literature, Honorary Fellow of
Balliol College, a Member of the Order of Ontario and a Companion of the
Order of Canada.

And then there are the honours he received for his work in theatre:
the Ottawa Drama League and the Gratien Gélinas prizes for play writing,
the Dominion Drama Award for production, and the Louis Jouvet trophy
for direction. His plays were praised for their humour, witty dialogue and
well-developed characters.

Despite his protestations that "I haven't any stories to tell.... I've just
worked all my life. Nobody wants to read about that ..,"*a major biography,
Robertson Davies: Man of Myth has just been published. Written by Judith
Skelton Grant, it records the life of a fascinating man.

William Robertson Davies was born in Thamesville, Ontario, on
August 28, 1913, the third son of Senator William Rupert Davies. He was
educated at Upper Canada College and Queen's University, and received
his B. Litt. from Balliol College, Oxford. After working at the Old Vic
Repertory Company in London, he returned to Canada in 1940 as literary
editor of *Saturday Night*. In 1942 he became editor of the *Peterborough
Examiner.*

During the forties and early fifties, Davies was our major Canadian
playwright; as well as writing, he both directed and produced his own and
other plays. He wrote his plays to entertain, rather than to proselytize. But
there is no doubt that his themes, in his plays and later in his novels, had an
impact on the development of Canadian cultural life, forcing Canadians to
consider the importance of the arts in a civilized country.

---

* From an interview with Stephen Smith, published in *Quill & Quire,* September 1994.

While continuing as publisher of the *Peterborough Examiner,* in 1960 he joined the faculty of Trinity College as a Visiting Professor. In 1963, he became the first Master of Massey College, a graduate college of University of Toronto. At that time he was appointed to the University of Toronto Faculty of English, and later the Drama Centre, where he taught Graduate courses in English and Drama until his retirement in 1981.

Selections from his newspaper columns formed the delightful Marchbanks books: *The Diary of Samuel Marchbanks, The Table Talk of Samuel Marchbanks* and *Samuel Marchbanks' Almanack.* Davies has become best known nationally and internationally for his thoughtful novels, with their Jungian overtones. His 1972 novel, *The Manticore,* won the Governor General's Award for Fiction. *What's Bred in the Bone,* published in 1985, was short-listed for the Booker Prize.

The Cunning Man, his eleventh novel, has just been published in 1994.